WORLD CHRISTIANITY, 1970-2000

Toward a New Millennium

Winston Crawley

William Carey Library
Pasadena, California

Published by
William Carey Library
P.O. Box 40129
Pasadena, CA 91114
(626) 798-0819
www.wclbooks.com

ISBN 0-87808-504-1

Printed in the United States of America

Dedicated
to
the theological seminaries
that have welcomed me to teach
and to
their devoted students

PREFACE

For several years, as guest professor of church history and/or the history of Christian missions in theological seminaries in the United States and in Asia, I have been interested in writing a survey of the Christian movement worldwide at the close of the millennium.

Dr. Ralph D. Winter has graciously encouraged me to proceed with this undertaking, as a successor to his earlier account of the progress of Christianity entitled *The Twenty-Five Unbelievable Years, 1945-1969.* Numerous friends and colleagues have also offered encouragement.

I want to express appreciation also for research assistance from Judith Bernicchi and Sandra Higgins of the Jenkins Research Library, and Jim Slack of the Global Research office at the Southern Baptist International Mission Board.

Winston Crawley
Richmond, VA
August, 2001

CONTENTS

INTRODUCTION

Advance Through Storm is the descriptive title that historian Kenneth Scott Latourette gave to the thirty-year period of Christian history from 1914 (the beginning of World War I) to 1944 (the year of completion of his seven-volume master work, *A History of the Expansion of Christianity).*[1] That "stormy" period included two world wars, the economic depression of the 1930s, the rise and spread of communism and fascism, plus undermining of Christian faith and missionary zeal by the spread of modern secular humanism. Even so, Latourette found clear evidence of Christian "advance."

Is Latourette's title for the early part of the century appropriate still for more recent years? Perhaps the storm has abated. Or perhaps Christian advance has slowed or even ceased.

Latourette's definitive account traced expansion of the Christian faith for more than nineteen centuries. He sought not merely to review the history of those centuries, but also to evaluate their events and movements, and to discern any pattern the history revealed. He incorporated his findings in several other books, some of them for more general readers. Latourette has been generally recognized as the primary authority on the history of world Christianity.

For many years I have admired and been greatly influenced by Latourette's work. One requirement of my doctoral studies in "The Theory and Practice of Missions" (which would now be called "Missiology") was to read all seven volumes of *A History of the Expansion of Christianity*. Latourette's interpretations and insights have become an integral part of my own thinking and teaching, both in the history of missions and in church history.

When some years had passed from the completion of Latourette's work, missiologist Ralph Winter produced a follow-up survey of the progress of world Christianity in *The Twenty-Five Unbelievable Years: 1945-1969.*[2] In an appendix, Winter briefly summarized Latourette's contributions, adding a long list of the books in which he presented his historical findings. Winter's updating of the story to 1969 has been well received and widely appreciated. A recent edition of *A History of the Expansion of Christianity* adds Winter's condensation of his own book as a supplement, thus recognizing it as a helpful addition to Latourette's history.

Now another thirty year period--often reckoned as one generation--has passed, bringing the 20th century to completion, and leading into a new millennium. This book, therefore, is its author's attempt to continue Latourette's and Winter's overview and analysis of current progress in world Christianity. As with Winter's work, this also makes no claim to the thoroughness with which Latourette described Christian history. It intends only to provide what may be a useful summary of the past thirty years, along the general lines laid out by Latourette.

As the title indicates, Christianity has been moving through the closing years of a millennium and toward the beginning of a new one. Although the eternal God presumably attaches little importance to human calculations of centuries and millennia, such concerns do become a factor in analysis and planning for people around the world--and thus are appropriate also in a study of the Christian movement in our day.

Latourette's evaluation of Christian progress focused on four criteria: numerical growth, geographic expansion, vitality as shown by new initiatives, and influence in society. Depending on the extent to which his review of historical events reflected increase or decrease in these measures, he judged the situation to be one of advance or decline for the Christian faith.

Latourette found in the centuries of Christian history a pattern of alternating advances and retreats. Each period of advance reached an ever higher level, and each retreat seemed briefer and less severe than the preceding one. The most impressive advance came during what Latourette called "The Great Century," from 1815 to 1914 (so impressive, in fact, that he devoted three of his seven volumes to that century).

After such amazing advance, would there be again in the years from 1914 to 1944 a time of retreat? Instead Latourette saw continuing advance--but in a time of multiplied difficulties, an "advance through storm."

Going back to the question with which this introduction began, what shall we say about the final thirty years of the millennium? Were they years of further advance or of retreat for world Christianity? We turn now to examine the record.

1

CONTEXT

The Christian faith (in contrast with many world religions) is distinctively historical, its essence inseparably tied to events in human experience. The Bible from its very beginning affirms the involvement of the transcendent God in earthly affairs. Thus biblical religion and the ongoing Christianity proceeding from it are inescapably interrelated with their historical context.

As an instrument for carrying out His purpose, God chose a special people. He took action through the major events of their history, such as the Exodus and the Exile. In those events, as indeed in the entire biblical story, God's people were related to the peoples around them and to the ebb and flow of kingdoms and empires. The story of the Chosen People can be understood only within the historical context of the Middle East across the centuries.

The incarnation of Christ is the centerpiece of Christian faith. It is God's affirmation of human life and human history. Followers of Jesus "are not of the world" but are "sent... into the world" (John 17:17-18 NIV). The earthly life of Christ and the experience of the early Church reflected and interacted with the society of the Mediterranean region. Again, that story can be understood only in light of its historical context. Indeed, the very concept of incarnation entails involvement with a very real world of human affairs.

The centuries of Christian history so fully recorded and analyzed by Latourette show also how greatly the expansion of Christianity has been affected by circumstances, for good and for ill. Obviously any examination of the Christian record during the past thirty years needs to give careful attention to all aspects of the setting for Christian life and work.

Context is always a crucial and sometimes a determinative factor in Christian history. In the first Christian century, for example, such elements as the Jewish *diaspora* and the pervasive Greco-Roman culture facilitated spread of the gospel in the Roman Empire. Centuries later, the growth and spread of Islam created a barrier to the expansion of Christianity. Latourette's account of Christian "advance through storm" cites many examples of the effects of context in the first half of the 20th century.

Expansion or contraction of the Christian faith are especially subject to powerful contextual influence. Political, religious, economic and social forces often limit the possibilities for gospel proclamation. Thus what can be done toward Christian outreach and advance depends on circumstances. An approach which may be fruitful in one situation may be entirely impossible in another.

Even where context places no serious limitations on Christian work, cultural factors affect decisions as to what should be done and how it should be done. Similarly, results of Christian efforts reflect the cultural setting. Persons in some situations respond to the gospel eagerly and rapidly, but response in other settings is hesitant and slow. Furthermore, the churches developing from Christian outreach show a wide variety of strengths and weaknesses, to a large degree representative of factors in their cultural environments.

We realize vividly, of course, that for the Christian faith context is neither primary nor final. God's purpose for His people holds primacy and will be fully and finally determinative. But in facing a new millennium, we Christians need clear understanding of the current world context for our lives and our Christian witness and ministries. We need to know what has been happening--and, in so far as possible, why it has happened, including the effects of the recent context.

Situation in 1970

One World--Views of the earth from space reinforced our awareness that we live in "one world." Communications theorist Marshall McLuhan in 1964 popularized the concept of the "global village." Though not achieved by 1970, it was already an impending world reality, becoming more fully actualized with each passing year.

Modern technology was the main factor in this apparent shrinking of the world. What has been called the Information Age was just dawning. (Integrated circuitry, which made computers smaller, less expensive, and almost ubiquitous, had been developed just in the 1960s.) But already rapid and convenient air travel and international telephone service, plus steady improvements in television, had brought the nations and continents much closer.

Interaction between regions that had once been complete strangers to one another had now become commonplace. The world had become more cosmopolitan, with a mixture of races, nationalities and religions in major cities everywhere--so that the kind of intercultural contacts that had once been rare were almost everyday occurrences.

International trade had made many national products prevalent around the world, and this trend was accelerated by the rise of more and more multi-national corporations, with a wider and wider reach. Though frequently resented and sometimes openly opposed, they seemed likely to flourish.

Some saw in the combined effects of these changes the evolution of a world culture, gradually overshadowing the differences in traditional cultures. However, closer examination seemed to show adoption of common elements mainly in material culture--with more basic aspects of cultures proving much more resistant to change.

Polarization--The obvious reality of a trend toward one world was counterbalanced by the equally obvious reality of division into rival and even enemy camps. The Cold War between capitalist and communist blocs that had followed World War II showed no signs of ending. The Atomic Age introduced in 1945 and the ensuing arms race had produced an uneasy standoff known as MAD (mutually assured destruction).

From time to time the Cold War had erupted into local hot wars, as in Korea in the early 1950s, and through insurrections in various parts of the world. In 1970, the long war in Vietnam continued to rage and had extended into Cambodia and Laos.

Chairman Mao's regime in China had reached a drastic new extreme through the Cultural Revolution that began in 1966. By 1970 its main thrust had ended, but it would continue to dominate all of life in China until 1976.

For several years it seemed that communism might be "the wave of the future" as more and more countries came under communist control. But by 1970 many observers began to wonder whether the movement had passed its peak. The alliance of China and the Soviet Union split in the 1960s. The trend toward communism in Indonesia was reversed in 1965. Soviet suppression of reform in Czechoslovakia in 1968 caused widespread disillusionment. And even in the Soviet Union the regime was less rigid and oppressive than in Stalin's days. Was the Cold War beginning to thaw?

Actually, alongside capitalist and communist worlds, there was also a "Third World." The term was widely used to designate "unaligned" nations, not clearly identified with either of the major groups engaged in the Cold War. Located mainly in Latin America, Africa and Asia, such nations were not as highly developed as the industrialized nations of the north and west. Many were young, having come to independence in the rapid de-colonizing after 1945 (what Ralph Winter described as "the retreat of the West").[3] By 1970 that segment of the world was growing in prominence, tentatively organizing to promote its interests, and playing an increasing role in world affairs.

Though now out of date, "Third World" may still be the most convenient, readily understandable term to encompass Latin America, Africa, and Asia. A major drawback is that some find it offensive. A possible alternative term, the "non-Western" world, has its own difficulties. (Donald McGavran coined a term, LATFRICASIA, which no one else adopted.) Recent evangelical jargon refers to the "Two-Thirds World"--

but the exact meaning is vague and it is not readily understood by outsiders. There is no entirely satisfactory simple way to speak collectively of Latin America, Africa, and Asia (plus sometimes also Oceania).[4]

Fragmentation--Countering the trend toward one world culture (and with due allowance for its political and economic varieties), the 1970 context included a powerful opposite trend, toward disunity and even fragmentation. Nationalism was the order of the day (a normal result of struggles for independence, and of the challenges of new nationhood). Within nations, cultural minorities were coming to heightened self-awareness and contending for recognition and new rights.

The natural outcome of these fresh aspirations, energized by strong leaders, was conflict in country after country, all around the world. In 1970, the Biafra war in Nigeria was just ending. The Palestine Liberation Organization was just rising to power (and being ejected by Jordan). Angola and Mozambique had not yet won independence from Portugal. Rhodesia and South Africa were controlled by white minorities. The Soviet Union was contending with "refuseniks" (Jews being hindered in their efforts to emigrate to Israel). Examples could be multiplied.

Demographics--The tensions and pressures of a troubled world were multiplied by rapidly increasing population, especially in the less developed countries of the so-called Third World. After centuries of relatively slow increase, world population had grown by an estimated 128 percent since 1900, to a total of roughly 3.7 billion.[5] (The annual growth rate was more than double the rate in the period from 1750 to 1900.)

Rapid improvements in medical care had reduced death rates, without comparable reduction in birth rates. Already there were concerns about a "population explosion" that might soon exceed food supply and revive the worst fears aroused by Malthus in the early 19th century. (Those concerns found graphic expression in Paul Ehrlich's book, *The Population Bomb*, published in 1968.)[6]

Intensifying urbanization also was critically changing the context for the Christian movement. By 1970, an estimated 37.4 percent of world population lived in cities.[7]
Populations in developed nations were rapidly "graying," while those in less developed lands were heavily weighted toward the younger age range.

Society--More than 40 percent of the world's nations had gained independence since 1945, and therefore in 1970 were still in the early stages of social, political and economic reconstruction. They were trying to develop their own patterns of government, to provide for educational and medical needs of their people, to build economies not dependent on colonialism, and to stimulate a sense of national identity--hindered often by ideological conflict and by tribal rivalries.[8]

In many and perhaps most cases, in response to what seemed intractable challenges, national leaders turned to authoritarian models--which then created new difficulties. Socialist policies (often influenced by Marxism) produced "planned economies." With many colonial powers having obstructed the training of indigenous leaders, and without prior experience in self-government, new nations struggled to find their way.

There were some notable successes. India, with all its handicaps, had become a functioning democracy--by far the largest in the world. Some new nations, especially on the

Pacific rim, were beginning to show economic gains. Japan, having recovered from crushing defeat in World War II, had become second in the world in Gross Domestic Product. Such progress was most evident in Asia, with Africa coming along more slowly. Latin America was not entirely comparable, since most nations there had been independent for more than a century, but some in 1970 were still wrestling with grave social, political and economic issues--most notably authoritarian governments and runaway inflation.

Meanwhile many Western nations had instituted various forms of "welfare states." There was increasing emphasis on guaranteeing civil rights for all segments of society. In the United States, partly in reaction against the Vietnam war, the 1960s had been a decade of social upheaval (marked by the assassinations of Martin Luther King Jr. and Robert Kennedy in 1968).

Contrasting emphases had been evident in the outreach into space (with the first human landing on the moon in 1969), and a more inwardly focused concern for our own planet's environment (with the first official "Earth Day" in 1970).

Religion--After what had seemed a time of general decline in the earlier part of the century, religions were showing new vitality by 1970.[9] Islam especially had realized resurgence in strength and expansion of influence.

According to researcher David Barrett, Christians numbered 33.5 percent of world population.[10] Barrett's figures report nominal adherents to all branches of Christian faith--including many, especially in the Western world, who are primarily "cultural Christians." (The same caution applies to figures for adherents of other religions.) The Christian total would likely have been higher except for efforts to suppress religion in communist countries. In such countries (and in most African and Asian countries) there would be little incentive for cultural Christianity.

Of the Christian total, Barrett's figures show 43.2 percent in the Western world, l6.0 percent in the communist world, and 40.7 percent in the Third World.

The Roman Catholic Church around the world was undergoing important changes as a result of the Vatican II conference held 1962-1965, changes primarily toward more liberal practices and more openness to modern life and to other Christians. Another influential development among Roman Catholics was liberation theology, which had originated in Brazil and was beginning to spread more widely.

Among Protestants, tension between opposing emphases on evangelism and social action was escalating (to reach its height in a Bangkok conference in 1973 and in responses to its theme).[11]

In two major ways the Christian movement of 1970 differed markedly from that of the early part of the century. One was the prominence of so-called "younger churches" (in the traditional "mission fields" of Asia and Africa). The other was the place of the charismatic movement, most impressively in Latin America.

On the whole, the religious situation was paradoxical, with strong anti-religious forces, with widespread secularism and materialism, and yet with new thrusts of religious vigor--

suggesting, in the familiar words of Dickens, "the best of times" and "the worst of times" for religion.

Meaning for Christianity--The Christian movement exists always in a real world, with possibilities conditioned by that world. At the entrance to the final thirty years of the 20th century, the world of 1970 was the church's context. How might that context affect the life and work of the church?

Much of what has been reviewed promised uncertainties and difficulties for the Christian faith. Though the "storm" identified by Latourette had moderated, it was not over. It was by no means certain that conditions would continue to moderate. The storm might escalate to even greater intensity. At the same time, much of what has been reviewed offered encouragement for increased spiritual opportunity--for greater openness and responsiveness to the Christian message. Indeed, troubled times often turn people's hearts to spiritual concerns. In 1970 that seemed a likely possibility in many parts of the world.

Most basically, perhaps, the 1970 context presented a major challenge to Christianity. How would Christians respond? Could they relate appropriately to a needy and troubled world? In some cases, spread of the faith faced "closed doors,"[12] which would require creative approaches. If Christianity could be true to its essence, there could be sympathetic understanding of human need and human aspirations, and an outpouring of compassionate ministries, properly adapted to the varying circumstances of a multi-faceted world.

Change, 1970-2000

Unusually rapid change has characterized the entire 20th

century. This has been true in all parts of the world, but especially in the highly developed West. Increasingly Western influence has brought change to other regions. It has become commonplace to think of revolutionary change as the central historical reality of the century, touching all aspects of human life (whether cultural, social, economic or political).

An easy way to visualize this change is by contrast with earlier centuries. For centuries, the daily life of most people in their rural villages changed very little from that of their ancestors. In this century, with improved communication and better educational opportunity, multiplied millions of persons even in remote locations have become aware of modern life in other places, and have begun to desire modern improvements for themselves. This awareness and desire fueled what observers came to call a "revolution of rising expectations."

The impact of radical change has caused what Alvin Toffler in 1970 called "future shock." He identified major characteristics of the changing situation as transience, novelty, and diversity. Persons everywhere in today's world must learn to adjust to these new conditions.[13]

In the final thirty years of the century, the rate of change accelerated. In some respects, its rapidity is almost unimaginable. Experts in information technology have asserted that the capacity of computer chips doubles about every 18-24 months. The Internet connects myriads of persons in all parts of the world. We hear of "human knowledge" multiplying at an amazing pace (though much "information" found on the Internet is of doubtful validity). Two computer disks by now, for example, can contain the entire content of the *Encyclopedia Brittanica*. Science textbooks, we are told, are out of date within about five years.

Although not as rapid as progress in the processing of information, improvements in transportation, communication, medicine, daily conveniences and other aspects of life occur at a dizzying pace.

By 1980, Toffler produced an update on modern change called *The Third Wave.*[14] John Naisbitt in 1982 gave similar attention to new directions in *Megatrends.*[15] He emphasized the shift from an industrial age to an information age, the "high tech" society, rise of a world economy, decentralization, and networking. A conference under United Nations sponsorship led to production of five volumes about challenges to global development, under the title *Change: Threat or Opportunity*. The volumes focus on political, economic, market, social, and ecological change.[16] These are examples of the many published surveys of current world transformation.

It is natural to wonder what such rapid change today may mean for the future. In fact, futurology is a rapidly growing field of study, reflected in hundreds of books and other reports.

Obviously such rapid change in its context in the past thirty years has called for continuing adjustment and readjustment as Christianity has responded to its environment.

Population Changes--A prominent element of change in the final decades of the 20th century was continuing rapid growth in world population, with increasing awareness that this could cause major problems if it persisted unabated. The first world conference on population was held in Romania in 1974. Paul and Anne Ehrlich in 1990 published *The Population*

Explosion,[17] a sequel to his 1968 book, *The Population Bomb.* While recognizing that earlier fears had moderated, they questioned whether there was sufficient current concern about the threat of mushrooming population.

Even more than in earlier decades, population expanded most rapidly in the poorer countries of the Third World, often called "developing countries." Hopes for improved quality of life were frequently frustrated by population growing more rapidly than resources could be multiplied by modern development.

Population pressures caused distortions in emerging economies. Though life expectancies increased, that took place mainly through reduced infant mortality. Thus many countries had demographic patterns overloaded with the young. In the 1990s it was reported that half the people in Kenya were under 15 years of age. (On the other hand, the graying of population in the Western world and in Japan accelerated.)

In rural settings, with continuing population growth, it obviously would be impossible to continue subdividing small plots of land between heirs and still pass down enough land to sustain all their families. Shifting to non-farm employment would be a possible remedy, if jobs could be created fast enough. Emigration in many cases became the actual alternate--and so persons from many less industrialized countries fled in large numbers to jobs in Western lands. (A prominent example was the large force of Turkish workers in Germany.)

During the time of near hysteria about the "population bomb" in the 1960s and early 1970s, some analysts had foreseen a crisis in food supply severe enough to require a "triage" approach, like that used in battlefield medical units: to divide the wounded into those who would survive regardless of medical help, those who would die anyway, and those for whom immediate medical help might make the difference between life and death. The world might need to judge which countries could be saved from famine, and focus help on those countries. But up to AD 2000 we have not encountered anything so disastrous.

One reason any critical food shortage has been delayed is the "green revolution"--rapid improvement in food crops and in agricultural methods. This was already beginning by 1970, and it has greatly augmented the world's supply of food. Hunger and malnutrition are still a basic everyday reality for millions of people, but massive famine is usually localized and temporary.

Another deterrent to an overpopulation crisis has been a decline in population growth rate, probably due largely to industrial and economic progress--but due at least in part to government efforts to encourage smaller families. In some cases governments have moved beyond promotion of birth control to coercion. The best known example is the "one-child" policy of the People's Republic of China. It has had not fully anticipated side effects: a disproportionate number of boy babies, and concern about emotionally "spoiled" children in many one-child families.

For a variety of reasons, including those just mentioned, the rate of population growth has slowed markedly in the past thirty years. In the early 1960s the growth rate estimated by the United Nations was 2.1 percent annually. By the 1990s the rate was only 1.4 percent. World population, however did exceed six billion by AD 2000--and unless we see further slowing of growth, that figure is expected to double by 2050. There remains serious question whether earth can support that many people without great tragedy.

Meanwhile, urbanization has continued apace. Cities have been growing at an annual rate at least twice that of the general population, which means that more than half of the growth of cities has come by persons moving in from rural areas.

Twenty to thirty years ago, United Nations demographers expected more than half the human race to live in urban settings by AD 2000. Barrett in 1986 foresaw a figure of 51.2 percent (compared with only 37.4 percent in 1970).[18] By now it is recognized that urban population has not grown quite that rapidly and it will be a few years yet before half the world's people are classified as urban..

Prominent in the urban scene has been the decline in relative size and importance of Western cities, as those in the developing world have grown much more rapidly. In 1970 New York was the world's largest city. By 1975 it was surpassed by Tokyo. And in the 1990s Mexico City took first place. Furthermore, of the world's 25 largest cities, eleven were in Europe and North America in 1970, and only four in AD 2000. Barrett describes this as the rise of "huge non-Christian supercities."[19]

Technology[20]--As noted earlier, scientific and technological advance, already so rapid earlier in the 20th century, continued unabated and even accelerated late in the century. Alongside the "population explosion" there was also a "knowledge explosion"--giving our day the label of the "Information Age." This unprecedented advance in recording and transmission of data came to be called "Information Technology" (IT).

Behind technological progress, though usually less noticed, was rapid advancement in basic scientific research, helped by massive grants for research and development (R & D) from industry, from higher education, and from governments. Discoveries in science, after a sufficient time lag, became developments in technology.

Probably most obvious, because now almost universal, is reliance on computers. As recently as 1970, there were probably fewer than 150,000 computers in use worldwide. Today the number runs in the hundreds of millions--and continues to multiply. Not only the absolute number of computers, but also their power grows exponentially. In accord with what is called "Moore's law," computer power has doubled every year and a half (or at most two years) during the past two decades.

Use of computers has facilitated, and often made possible, major improvements in other aspects of life. Exploration of space would have been well nigh impossible without computers. Though ventures in space have seemed less spectacular since the initial moon landing in 1969, some activities in space have become almost commonplace: surveillance and communication satellites, probes sent throughout our solar system, space stations and the American space shuttle going back and forth, plus international cooperation. People have begun to speculate about visiting or vacationing in space.

Genetics has become another area of major scientific and techno-logical progress. Genetic engineering is now a reality, though a disputed one, in agriculture. The cloning of a sheep in 1996 caught public attention everywhere. Most important for the future was completion of the mapping of the human genome at the end of the century.

For most people the most welcome scientific and technological advances have been medical. New drugs are being developed and tested constantly, bringing hope for relief to many sufferers. Many ancient scourges have been driven back, prolonging life expectancy in all parts of the world. A notable example was the final elimination of smallpox in 1978. New treatment procedures and the latest equipment produce miracles. After the first heart transplant surgery in 1967, such procedures were used more and more, with increasing effectiveness. By the end of the century there had been more than 20,000 successful heart transplants; and transplants of kidneys, livers, lungs, and other body parts are no longer startling.

Communication possibilities at the end of the century, however, still amaze. Television shows us events as they happen on the opposite side of the world. After Nelson Mandela was released from prison in South Africa in 1990, he traveled widely. To his surprise, in Alaska he met Innuit young people who had seen his release on television. The computer Internet is even more astonishing. From bare beginnings in the late 1960s, it has spread worldwide and has been doubling annually since 1988 in number of persons involved and in data transmitted .

The conveniences and the possibilities of everyday life are enhanced constantly by technology we hardly notice (for example, the scanners in supermarkets, or the weather reports readily on call on radio or television). We depend on electronic controls for our cars and our household devices, our cameras, and a myriad of other implements. Furthermore, this intensified use of technology has been spreading rapidly through the entire world, with the vastly greater awareness it brings to people everywhere.

Such remarkable and rapid change brings both promise and threat. Life can become much better for everyone. But science and technology can also bring new problems and dangers. One growing concern in our day, for example, is potential major damage to earth's environment. Because of the chance of either benefit or harm, or perhaps both, from many changes outlined above, such changes give rise to new ethical challenges. It seems we have not progressed as rapidly or as far in ethical judgments and in social responses as we have in science and technology.

Political Developments--Most momentous of all the changes in the past thirty years has been the surprising and radical transformation of the political setting. The communist world had seemed almost monolithic and quite formidable. Although some cracks had begun to appear earlier, the unexpected fall of the Berlin wall in 1989 gave startling symbolism to the impending disintegration of the system. By the end of 1991, the Soviet Union dissolved and what President Reagan had called the "evil empire" disappeared.

This amazing outcome meant the end of the Cold War, which had dominated international relations for nearly half a century. The atomic threat of "mutual assured destruction" (with its acronym, MAD) diminished. For the major world powers, large sums which had been spent for munitions could now be redirected toward meeting human needs. Of course the new configuration of the world brought novel problems, which would require world leaders to give much time and effort toward their solution. We are still living amid that struggle to define and cope with international relations in the post-Cold War setting.

The decline of Soviet power brought transformation to Soviet satellite states in eastern Europe. In 1990, East and West Germany reunited. Poland had already gained a measure of autonomy through the success of its Solidarity movement. Struggles for control, communist versus non-communist, erupted in other lands--with varying degrees of carry-over from the old regimes. Yugoslavia began to fall apart. The Baltic nations regained their independence. Freedom of movement and free flow of information became facts of life throughout the region.

Disbandment of the Soviet Union created many new countries in eastern Europe and in central Asia. Belarus, the Ukraine, and Moldova, which had been Soviet Socialist Republics in the USSR, became separate nations. Five central Asian republics and three in the Caucasus region won nationhood. Though these joined in a loose confederation, the Commonwealth of Independent States (CIS), it had little authority. Even Russia itself entered an extended period of internal disorder, striving toward its own pattern for a more free and democratic society.

Communism was also losing much of its clout elsewhere, or at least declining in rigidity and totalitarian control. Mongolia, for example, turned toward democracy. Ethiopia, Angola, and Mozambique backed away from earlier communist domination. Albania ended communist rule. Even Cuba moderated its stance, and North Korea began opening to the rest of the world.

The People's Republic of China, the other major communist power, did not renounce its ideology. It gained admittance to the United Nations in 1971. Later, however, it did undergo great change. After the end of the Cultural Revolution and the death of Chairman Mao in 1976, and following a period of strife, Deng Xiaoping took control. His policies aimed at modernization, to be accompanied by new openness to the Western world and by increasing freedom internally. But the limits to his tolerance were shown by disastrous events at Tiananmen Square in Beijing in 1989. The ruling party was determined to maintain its power. Its image of severity was somewhat mitigated, however, by its agreement to a "one country, two systems" plan for the reunion of Hong Kong with China in 1997.

Historian Arnold Toynbee has been reported as saying that he did not expect a third world war in the final half of the 20th century--but that he did expect many localized "brush fire" wars. That certainly has been the case, with usually many such armed clashes at the same time in different parts of the world. Some have been international, but most have been civil strife between competing ideologies or social groups. As the century progressed, United Nations peace-keeping forces became a more and more familiar element in conflict situations. A most disturbing feature of recent clashes has been widespread terrorism, directed against non-combatants for strategic purposes, and even occasional genocide.

The most visible local war, in Vietnam, had already been under way for years before 1970, and had involved the United States heavily, and several other nations to a lesser extent. It finally ended in 1975, with the nation unified under the communist government based in Hanoi. A flood of refugees ensued, many on makeshift boats. Withdrawal of American forces from the region opened the way for communist victory also in Laos and Cambodia. A new government in Cambodia proved especially vicious, and refugees flooded across the border to Thailand to escape genocide in their homeland.

Conflict between modernizing and reactionary elements in Iran led to the ousting of the Shah in 1979. Revolutionaries seized the American embassy and held its occupants captive until early 1981.

Ethno-nationalism (in some cases little more than tribalism) has sparked and fueled most of the recent wars. Probably the most significant was that which formed the nation of Bangladesh in 1971. More recent strife in Rwanda, in Bosnia, in Kosovo and in scores of other places has captured world attention and world concern.

The Middle East is an arena of seemingly irreconcilable struggle, with Arab states and especially the Palestine Liberation Organization ranged against Israel, and each side determined to achieve its aims. From the Yom Kippur war in 1973 on to the *intifada* in the 1990s, and despite multiplied attempts to find a formula for agreement, the struggle continues.

The Persian Gulf war in 1991, perhaps surprisingly, arrayed a number of Arab states alongside Western powers (and the United Nations) against Iraq, which had invaded and captured Kuwait. The war restored the freedom of Kuwait, but tension with Iraq over possible "weapons of mass destruction" persists.

In spite of much contention and some setbacks, the past thirty years have seen a surge of increasing personal freedom in most of the world. A prominent example is the ending of *apartheid* in South Africa by 1994. Furthermore, many nations have moved toward more democratic systems of government (as, for example, in the ending of military dictatorships in many South American countries). The global political situation and outlook, though far from ideal, have become far more favorable than in 1970.

Economic Progress--Globalization has been the outstanding economic feature of recent history. Many factors have contributed to the ongoing development of an interconnected world economy. Better transportation and communication were earlier influences. Reduced international tensions also helped. These changes led to greatly augmented trade. Multinational enterprises mushroomed. And more recently computers, and especially the Internet, have linked the world into a vast electronic network. Thus planners today can ill afford to ignore the impact of globalization on their enterprises.

On the whole, the world's economy is better than in 1970. Average per capita income (adjusted for inflation) is higher. For most of the world, "quality of life" has improved. But economic progress has been uneven, and poverty is endemic in many places. The *International Human Suffering Index*[21] shows much of Africa still lagging in economic development and the betterment it can provide. David Barrett's *World Christian Encyclopedia* includes an impressive graphic summary of human need worldwide,[22] and Frank Caleb Jansen's *Target Earth* describes various kinds of need at length.[23]

A strong trend toward economic freedom has been evident in recent years. In part this has reflected the decline in communism and its "central planning." But similar changes have taken place in the West and in much of the non-Western world. Even the People's Republic of China, though retaining centralized political control, has allowed a relatively free economy. Where a "market economy" has been instituted, economic progress has seemed to follow (though with many accompanying adjustment problems).

Regional organizations for economic cooperation have become common, in North America and in the Pacific basin, for example, and most notably in Europe. The European Economic Community (EEC), which had been founded in 1957, evolved in 1987 into the European Union (EU), which by 1999 had its own currency, the euro.

Asia has experienced especially dramatic economic change in recent decades. Japan became an outstanding player on the world scene--though its own economy then ran into trouble in the early 1990s. Four emerging Asian economies grew so rapidly as to be called the "Four Tigers" (Korea, Taiwan, Hong Kong, and Singapore)--but they also encountered problems in the mid-1990s. Under the leadership of Deng Xiaoping, China's economy boomed.

Though the overall picture has been favorable, there have been economic problems. "Oil shocks" in 1973-74 and in 1979-80 caused difficulties especially for industrialized countries, and fluctuating oil prices are still troubling. Several lands of Europe found their "welfare states" hard to finance and had to make adjustments. Newly adopted market economies could not produce immediate miracles, since it takes time to build up economic strength--and impatient populaces found it hard to wait. Tensions have escalated between the more industrialized "North" and the "South."

International debt was seen as a looming crisis by the end of the century. Many poor nations were carrying an oppressive load of debt to richer nations, or mainly to international organizations. Campaigns for debt relief were gaining widespread support. With so many strong economies, there was a growing movement for increased help to those economies that were still struggling.

Social/Cultural Change--In the early and middle years of the 20th century, the world seemed moving toward cultural oneness. The spread of Western culture throughout the world, which had been accelerated by colonialism, was changing life everywhere--most notably in cities and among educational and business leaders. To be sure, adaptation was not just a one-way street. The emerging world culture included elements from many lands. The West itself was showing increased influence from the East.

Late in the century, however, an opposing trend became evident--a decentralizing tendency. People everywhere began to reassert their ethnic identities, reclaiming their distinctive languages or dialects and cultural heritage. In many cases this involved open resistance to encroachments of Western culture. Superficial elements of modern material development might be accepted, but the roots of worldview and customs often remained almost untouched. Even the Western world itself displayed the same recovery of ethnicity, with its fragmenting effects.

Meanwhile, Western culture has undergone what is proclaimed as a fundamental paradigm shift, from the modern rational and scientific understanding which had been dominant for almost three centuries to a new "postmodern" view. This current philosophy questions the possibility of objective certainty about anything and everything. Though it began a few decades ago in the rarefied atmosphere of European academia, its basic viewpoint has now spread widely through Western culture. One effect has been to reinforce those aspects of European life and thought which were already considered post-Christian. Influences of the postmodern paradigm on society today are largely unconscious, since only a small minority are philosophically literate, but ideas and attitudes that reflect such views have become commonplace.

Contemporary media are the prime vehicle for silent spread of a new worldview and related concepts. Increasingly as the century progressed, the communicative power of the press and of electronic media, including the Internet, permeated our world. Television as a medium is especially suited to the postmodern perspective, with its emphasis on direct personal experience.

As we move into a new century, many ominous social challenges confront us. Some of the most serious arise from the demographic, political, and economic realities already described: escalating needs of the elderly in some settings, and the pressing demands of youth in others; genocidal conflicts, with their floods of refugees; dire poverty, malnutrition, and disease. Added to these are the current plagues of drug abuse, most notably in Western nations, and AIDS, most drastically in Africa. Further current issues include crime, abortion, and threats to family life.

Racism is a serious, continuing, worldwide problem. Though laws in many countries now prohibit its worst manifestations, they are insufficient to change attitudes rooted in long-standing tradition. Inter-racial conflicts frequently involve political, economic, and religious factors. Thus such conflicts resist any easy solution. (Hostility in Israel between Jews and Arabs is typical.)

Human rights have gained increasing emphasis in recent years. The Helsinki Declaration of 1975, adopted by 35 countries and given implicit recognition by many more, helped to provide a standard with international backing. Actual practice, of course, has fallen far below that standard. Still it serves as a challenge for ongoing progress toward protection of human rights everywhere.

Another vital current concern, preserving the environment, has become a popular icon. This has prompted formal studies of ecology, and international conferences to discuss and propose appropriate actions. Possible human influence on global warming is a special focus of concern. While Western nations show increasing desire to place controls or limits on whatever may harm the environment, many less industrialized nations would give priority to the freedom needed for their own development.

Religion--The closing years of the 20th century have been a time of religious renewal. The growing religious energy noted in 1970 had become even more evident by AD 2000. In many lands, relaxation of communist controls on religion has provided still further opportunity for increased religious activity.

This revival (often described as a "renaissance") of religion has manifested itself in many ways. People of various lands and faiths have become more obviously "religious"--more open in religious allegiance and activities. In the Western world, many persons have adopted a vague spirituality, without much definition of belief or consistency of practice, and often averse to formal organization (such as churches). New religious movements have sprung up all over the world, some sanctifying common elements of local culture, and others going counter to cultural norms.

The world's religious situation has become more and more mixed, as millions of people have left their homelands (for a variety of reasons) and moved to distant lands. Whereas in earlier centuries mapping the locations of religions was fairly simple, that is no longer the case. It is still possible to produce such a map--but with stated cautions that there is much overlapping and that boundaries shown are "partly arbitrary."[24]

Population movements and other religious changes have made it increasingly difficult to get reliable statistics on religions. To a large extent, reported increases in adherents to the different religions have reflected population growth rates in those regions where the religions predominate.

Intermixing of cultures and religions has helped stimulate religious relativism, especially in the West and among intellectual elites worldwide. Such relativism (or "pluralism") also fits well with today's postmodern views.

An opposite reaction, resisting any watering down of religious convictions, has generated fundamentalist movements in the major religions. These have in some cases become extremist, even to the extent of using terrorism to further their aims. Resulting conflicts, though including intense religious motivation, often involve also ethnic, cultural, political, and economic factors. Where a nation has a traditional religion, fundamentalism may breed fanatical religious nationalism, with discrimination against and persecution of minority religious groups.

2

GROWTH AND SPREAD

Latourette's exhaustive survey and analysis focused on the *expansion* of the Christian faith, both numerical and geographical. Our knowledge about the status of world Christianity can never be complete or flawless, but available information can give a fairly accurate picture of general trends, clear and thorough enough for our evaluation.

David Barrett, recognized as the outstanding Christian researcher of our day, provides by far the most comprehensive and reliable data on religions. He produced the original *World Christian Encyclopedia* in 1982 and the two-volume Second Edition (with associates) in early 2001. These offer unbelievably thorough information on religions and especially on Christianity, both for the world as a whole and country by country. Since 1985 Barrett has produced brief annual updates, carried in January issues of the *International Bulletin of Missionary Research.*

Numbers

Growth in numbers can be evaluated in absolute terms (as an attempt to count the Christians in the world) and also in relative terms (as a percentage of world population).

As a researcher, Barrett deals with measurable indicators.

Thus his numbers for all religions report nominal adherence. There is no way to measure spiritual reality--how sincere, how well informed, or how earnest one's religious commitment may be. For Christianity the numbers include all who may consider themselves to be Christians in any sense, or may be so considered by society. Still these figures can suit our purposes: since their criteria are consistent from place to place and from time to time, they give reasonably reliable evidence of growth or of decline.

The number of Christians in the world (by Barrett's broad definition) has been growing rapidly, from an estimated 1.236 billion in 1970 to approximately 2 billion in 2000. The average annual growth rate has been 1.62 percent. This compares to a rate of 1.14 percent between 1900 and 1970. Numerical growth of Christianity has accelerated markedly since 1970.

Comparing the number of Christians to population is much more complex--especially if the comparison is intended as evidence of actual Christian strength. For perspective on this problem, we can examine Barrett's data for the earlier part of the century. For AD 1900 he shows Christians as 34.4 percent of world population, but only 33.5 percent by 1970. On a relative basis, Christianity apparently was declining. In explanation, Barrett pointed to secularism in western Europe, communism in Russia and eastern Europe, and materialism in North America.

Was that an actual decrease in Christian strength? When persons who call themselves Christians for social or cultural reasons cease to do so, it is not necessarily a loss to the Christian faith. It may indeed help clarify the essence of the faith. For example, after Russia became communist, being "Christian" no longer had social or cultural value, but instead involved difficulties and danger. Millions of "Christians" decided to drop any claim to faith, thus shifting to the "nonreligious" category in Barrett's tables. (If Russia had shown as large a percentage Christian in 1970 as in 1900, the percentage of Christians for the world would have shown an increase of almost 1 percent rather than a decline.)

Barrett again showed a decline between 1970 and 2000 in the ratio of Christians to world population, from 33.5 to 33.0 percent. As in the pre-1970 decades, Christian gains in the Third World were overbalanced by losses in the West. That was due in part to lower birth rates in the nominally Christian West than in primarily non-Christian regions (which would result in a gradually decreasing Christian proportion of total population). More telling, however, was what Barrett calls continuing "defection" from Christianity (nominal, that is).

If we are concerned not merely for growth in numbers, but perhaps even more for growth in real strength, other categories in Barrett's tables may be more revealing. Evangelicals show an increase from 2.5 to 3.5 percent of world population between 1970 and 2000. Barrett lists also a fairly new category which he calls "Great Commission Christians," defined as follows:

> Believers in Jesus Christ who are aware of the implications of Christ's Great Commission, who have accepted its personal challenge in their lives and ministries, are attempting to obey his commands and mandates, and who are seeking to influence the body of Christ to implement it.[25]

For this category, Barrett reports a striking increase, from 7.5

percent of world population in 1970 to 10.7 percent in 2000. Such addition to a committed central core of Christians reveals vibrant growth in the true strength of world Christianity.

Geography

Along with growth in numbers, the Christian faith has continued its spread throughout the world. Barrett in the introduction to the Second Edition of his *Encyclopedia* refers to "Christians and organized churches in every inhabited country" by AD 2000. But he also notes that "spread is very uneven."[26] In two-thirds of the 238 "countries" analyzed, Christians are a majority of the population. In 84 countries the proportion is more than 90 percent. On the other hand, there are 14 countries in which Christians of any kind number less than 1 percent of the total.

Growth of Christianity since 1970 has varied greatly from place to place, with quite rapid growth in some regions and especially in a few countries, but with the number of Christians in some cases failing to keep up with increasing population--or perhaps even with net numerical losses.

Among the continents, by Barrett's count, the most striking decline in proportion to population was in North America--from 91.3 percent Christian in 1970 to only 84.2 percent in 2000. Latin America also shows a loss in Christian percentage of population, with enough "defection" of nominal Roman Catholics to more than outnumber the significant gains by Protestants and evangelicals, and especially by Pentecostals.

Europe would have shown a declining percentage Christian, with the continuing trend to secularism in Western Europe, except for the great number of persons reclaiming Christian faith (primarily Orthodox) in Eastern Europe after the ending of communist rule. In Russia the Christian percentage moved from 38.4 to 57.4, and in the Ukraine from 60.0 to 83.0. The increase in Albania was more remarkable, from 8.1 to 35.4 percent. Christian percentages for Europe as a whole were 75.1 in 1970 and 76.8 in 2000.

Major growth for Christianity occurred in Africa, with 1.5 million net additional believers per year (and Christian ratio for the entire continent up from 40.3 to 45.9 percent). Countries where the percentage increase was most striking were in eastern Africa (Uganda, Kenya, Tanzania, Malawi, and Mozambique) and in south central Africa (Zambia and Zimbabwe). Nigeria had a large numerical increase in Christians, but with base numbers already so big, a strong percentage increase was unlikely.

Asia also showed good Christian growth, with 2.4 million net additional believers per year. For the continent, the ratio of Christians was 4.7 percent in 1970 and 8.5 percent in 2000. Countries where Christianity grew amazingly included Armenia after the breakup of the Soviet Union (34.1 percent to 84.0 percent), Nepal (.1 to 2.4), Thailand (1.0 to 2.2), and South Korea (18.3 to 40.8). Although the rate of growth is not as impressive, the size of the populace in India gives special weight to the increase in Christians there, from 4.2 to 6.2 percent. That is true on a smaller scale of Indonesia, with its increase from 10.3 to 13.1 percent.

The People's Republic of China was the site of the most spectacular growth of Christian faith, the greatest spiritual miracle of the 20th century. In 1970 the Cultural Revolution, though considered officially ended, was still dominant. Churches had been closed, and many Christian leaders were imprisoned or exiled to work camps. Open religious activity was forbidden. But Christians still met in families or small informal gatherings. The outside world had little knowledge of that situation in China, and lack of public records meant that only estimates of Christian presence were possible. Barrett estimated Christians at 1,515,000 or .2 percent of China's population.

In 1979, under policies instituted by Deng Xiaoping, religion gained limited freedom, and the outside world began to learn more about conditions in China. For 1980, Barrett reported 1,800,000 Christians in China. But information from China soon showed a much larger and rapidly expanding Christian movement. Did all this growth begin suddenly after the easing of government pressures? It seems more likely that much had gone on already, behind the scenes and quietly, during the closing years of severe repression. Not until 1979 could the growth begin to be seen.

As early as 1985 Barrett mentioned having seen exaggerated estimates of up to 98 million Christians in China![27] Two years later he himself was using a figure of 52,152,000 and describing it as "the fastest expanding nation for church growth ever."[28] Rapid increase is continuing. For AD 2000 Barrett reports a total of 89,055,551 Christians in China, 7.1 percent of China's people.

Freedom vs. Restriction

Extension and growth of Christianity reflect the varying degrees of freedom for religious activity in different places. In general, greater freedom is conducive to greater growth. But the correlation if not exact. Sometimes remarkable growth occurs in situations of severe restriction (as just described in China). And sometimes conditions of complete freedom lead to no Christian growth, or perhaps even decrease.

For several decades, church and missions leaders have lamented "closed countries"--that is, nations which do not welcome missionaries from outside, seeing such restriction as a prime hindrance to the spread of the gospel. Missiologist Ralph Winter has called that "the myth of closed countries," implying that the problem is nowhere near as severe as the term suggests.

Of course no country can close itself to the presence of God. And even when entry of foreign missionaries is limited, Christians within the country often have much freedom. Assistance for the Christian cause across national borders can take many forms, such as prayer, broadcasting, literature, fraternal visits, aid projects, or workers who are not technically "missionaries." Thus any impression that countries are closed to Christian witness and ministry is only a myth.

Nevertheless, it remains true that the extension, the growth, and the strength of the Christian faith are often affected greatly by the degree of freedom or limitation. Under Soviet Union control of Eastern Europe and much of Asia, as we have noted, Christians (at least in the nominal sense) decreased greatly in those areas. When Soviet control ended, reported Christians grew rapidly--and large numbers of missionaries from other lands were allowed to enter to help spread and strengthen the faith.

There still are large areas of the world which place stringent limitations on Christian witness and ministry, with the result that the faith grows only slowly in such areas.

Actual persecution of Christians intensifies the problem. Secular Western society, though it has become quite sensitive to discrimination in many forms, still gives little attention to often ruthless persecutions in other parts of the world. Martyrdom, far from being the rarity that most might expect, is a pervasive reality of Christian experience in too many lands.

The *World Christian Encyclopedia* has analyzed Christian martyrdoms across the centuries. It identifies martyrs by five criteria: "believers in Christ, who have lost their lives, prematurely, in situations of witness, as a result of human hostility."[29] Despite serious effort to apply these criteria strictly, the totals seem overstated at points by counting as martyrs persons who happened to be of the wrong ethnic group in the wrong place or at the wrong time. (For example, Rwanda genocide in 1994 was more ethnic and political than religious.) Some observers are quite skeptical of Barrett's figures.[30] Even with reservations as to probable overstatement, the numbers reported are staggering.

Perhaps largely because there are so many more Christians today, the *Encyclopedia* notes more martyrdoms in the 20th than in any previous century. However, the rate has been declining. In the first half of the century, the rate reported was about 640,000 per year, and in the second half only 278,000. Currently (leading up to AD 2000), the annual rate is down to 160,000. Increasing freedom may be a factor in the improvement. Perhaps increasing world attention to persecution is also a restraining influence.

People Groups

Prior to 1970, summary evaluations of Christian progress paid relatively little attention to population subgroups, reporting mainly in terms of nations and their political subdivisions. That was true even of the initial *World Christian Encyclopedia*, published in 1982. Through a process to be described later (Chapter 5), people groups became a major concern of missions agencies and of many Christian leaders and workers.

Greatest interest centered on "peoples" (that is, people groups) which had not been evangelized. After agreement on how to define such peoples and research to identify them, the next step would be specific plans by mission agencies for Christian witness and ministry to the "unreached peoples," and for planting churches among them. The past thirty years have seen significant progress.

In the 1990s, what was called the Joshua Project identified about 1,600 "least reached peoples" (groups of more than 10,000 persons, with relatively limited Christian presence). According to project reports, between 1990 and 2000 the proportion of such peoples with church planting teams on site increased from 39 percent to 68 percent. Evangelists participating in a global convocation at Amsterdam during the year 2000 pledged themselves to work toward reaching what were reported as the final 253 unreached peoples. Thus, by the century's end, missions agencies were projecting plans to send church planting teams to such peoples, with target dates no later than mid-2002.

Even with the best efforts of many researchers and missions agencies, it has been difficult to know exactly the status of the Christian faith in all of the perhaps 13,000 ethno-linguistic peoples of the world. The Joshua Project report just cited gives at least a general view of remarkable expansion of the faith into groups that earlier included few or no Christians.

Evangelization

Influence of the Christian movement extends far beyond those persons who are themselves identified as Christian. Additional millions have some awareness and understanding of the faith. Thorough evaluation of Christian progress in the past thirty years needs to include some estimate of the ongoing spread of knowledge of the gospel (now usually called "evangelization").

As in the case of Christian faith itself, evangelization is hard to measure. When has a person "heard" the gospel in a meaningful sense? Various answers are possible. Most authentic would be hearing with enough cultural and personal relevance to produce understanding and enable a response of faith. But that is a matter of inner, spiritual reality which cannot be quantified. By such a realistic definition, only rough approximations are possible.

As a researcher and statistician, David Barrett has developed a scheme for analyzing the availability of information about the gospel. Of course this does not mean that every person where the message is available has actually heard and understood. Barrett's figures, though, do provide a basis for comparisons between places and for estimates of change with the passing of time. By Barrett's broad definition, 55.6 percent of world population had been "evangelized" by 1970--that is, lived in places where the gospel was "available."

The gospel has spread rapidly since 1970. New attention to

people groups has made the message available in formerly untouched regions. The Bible has been translated, in whole or in part, into more and more languages. By 2000, the United Bible Society was reporting some portion of the Scriptures available in 2,261 languages (an increase of 28 languages in just the previous 12 months). It is estimated that 94 percent of the world's people now have at least the New Testament in their own tongue. Languages with Christian broadcasting increased from less than 100 in 1970 to more than 350 by 2000.

An especially effective project, the *Jesus* film produced by Campus Crusades and based on the Gospel of Luke, by 1999 had been translated into 547 languages or dialects. An estimated 2.9 billion persons had seen the film.

With the Christian message being made more and more widely available in these and other ways, Barrett's estimate for the "evangelized" portion of the world is up to 73.1 percent by 2000, a most impressive extension of Christian influence on the world.

3

CENTER OF GRAVITY

Through twenty centuries of history, the areas where Christian strength is mainly concentrated have shifted several times. Recent observers have described such changes as shifts in the "center of gravity" of the Christian faith. They do not take place suddenly, but over a period of time--usually at least several decades, and perhaps a century or more. Such changes are usually most clearly evident only after they are well under way, or even completed.

During its early centuries, until the Roman Empire expired, Christianity centered in the Mediterranean world. To be sure, it extended well beyond that region and that empire, but its greatest numbers and greatest strength (by almost any measure) were concentrated in lands surrounding the Mediterranean Sea. There was its center of gravity.

AD 476 is the recognized date for the end of the Roman Empire, though the effects of its decline and fall both preceded and followed that year. Loss of centralizing political power and incursions of barbarian tribes, sweeping across Europe and as far as North Africa, led to what Latourette called "a thousand years of uncertainty" for Christianity--and what historians have often called the "Dark Ages" in Europe. Islam arose in the 7th century and soon took control of the Middle East and North Africa, causing major declines in Christian faith in those areas, and cutting European contact with Africa and Asia. Europe thus became the main region in which it was possible for Christianity to expand and grow strong.

From at least as early as the 7th century, Europe was the center of gravity for Christianity. That situation continued for more than a thousand years, well past European discovery of the Americas and of sea routes around Africa to Asia. As a result, the rest of the world came to consider Christianity a European religion.

In the 19th century and the first half of the 20th century, North America developed enough Christian strength to be associated with Europe as the combined stronghold of the faith. As recently as 1970, the two continents comprising the heart of the Western world were still clearly the center of gravity for Christianity. Of world Christians, 56.9 percent lived in those continents. Most treatments of theology and church history, even those studied in the non-Western world, were basically "European" in thought forms, content, and emphases. The most prominent Christian institutions were based in the West, as was the growing mission movement which was sharing Christianity worldwide.

As the 20th century drew nearer to its close, the situation was changing. Recent decades have shown the beginning of a major shift in the Christian center of gravity. It is not yet complete and may not be so for many more decades--but it is well under way and appears irreversible. The heartland of Christianity, located in Europe for more than a millennium (with North America recently added), seems sure in the 21st century to be found in what we have called the Third World (or Two-Thirds World).

World Christianity 1970-2000

Numbers

On the most superficial level, numbers themselves reflect the change: the majority of Christians now live outside Europe and North America. By AD 2000, in a period of only thirty years, percentages of Christians in the traditional center and the newly developing center more than reversed, with 59 percent by now in Latin America, Africa, Asia, and Oceania. (up from only 43.1 percent in 1970).

This is not a sudden development. Its arrival was visible even by 1970. Walbert Buhlmann in the 1970s wrote of the "coming of the Third Church"--the church of the Third World and the third millennium--in which Christians of Latin America, Africa, and Asia would set the agenda for the whole church. By the early 1980s he wrote (with special reference to Roman Catholics):

> What is effectively the centre of gravity of Christianity... has shifted more and more, and 1970 reached a critical point: by then 51 percent of all Catholics were living in the southern continents: Latin America, Africa, Asia-Oceania. Until 1980 the proportion went on rising to 57.76 percent. By the year 2000 a good 70 percent of all Catholics will be living in the southern hemisphere.[31]

Protestant and evangelical observers were foreseeing the same kind of change, but evidence has become much stronger as time has passed.

Theology

Transition to a new Christian center of gravity involves a flow of increasingly prominent and influential theological ideas and systems from the non-Western world. They reflect a background quite different from that of traditional Western

Christianity. As early as 1976, Gerald Anderson and Thomas Stransky recognized and reinforced that development by publishing *Mission Trends No. 3: Third World Theologies.* Their foreword stated:

> A radical theological realignment is taking place in the Church today. The old centers of theological influence in Europe and North America are becoming the new peripheries. The new centers of vitality and importance in theological construction are in Asia, Africa, and Latin America.... Ironically, this fact... is not yet widely recognized or understood in the old centers. There is still a good deal of theological provincialism.[32]

Provincialism has not entirely vanished, but recognition of Third World theologies has become much more widespread and more appreciative. In the meantime, Third World theologians have developed an awareness of their distinctiveness, shown in the forming of the Ecumenical Association of Third World Theologians in 1976.

Probably the most influential (and certainly the best known) theological movement from the Third World is liberation theology. It began before 1970, but its main spread and influence came in the 1970s and 1980s. Originating among Roman Catholics in Latin America, it soon affected theological thought not only in other similar political and economic settings, but also in European and North American centers of traditional theology. It is a prime example of emerging worldwide interaction in Christian thinking and writing.

Because Christians in Africa and Asia are in constant, direct, and intimate relation with cultures molded by other religions, their theologies inevitably reflect the existence of other religious beliefs and practices. As our world has become more cosmopolitan, such concerns have come to be understood as a basic element in theology. Early in the century, most Western treatments of systematic theology included no reference to other religions. By now, a section expounding a theology of religions is an expected part of any complete theology.

Missions

An especially significant and even amazing expression of the shift in Christian center of gravity has been the recent rapid expansion of mission outreach originating in and projected from lands that formerly had been considered only as mission fields.

Such outreach is not entirely new. Much of the evangelizing of Oceania was done by Pacific islanders, beginning as early as the 1820s and including eventually more than a thousand Pacific island missionaries. On a smaller scale, Christians of many Asian, African, and Latin American countries went as missionaries to other lands long before 1970. However, during most of the modern missionary movement (generally dated from William Carey and 1792), Europe and North America (supplemented more recently by other "Western" lands like Australia, New Zealand, and South Africa) produced the vast majority of international missionaries.

It was still appropriate in 1974 for Peter Wagner to ask, "What color are missionaries' feet?" and to follow with the comment, "When you think of all those missionary feet going out, what color feet do you see? Probably white!" That still was the common perception, and it was substantially accurate. But that picture was changing, and would change more and more rapidly. As Wagner suggested, "These white feet will be joined by a vastly increasing number of brown, black, red and yellow feet."[33]

Mission efforts based in former mission "fields" gradually gained wider attention, with a growing general awareness of their contribution to the total world mission. Several survey reports and articles on the subject appeared in the early 1960s. The first careful, worldwide research was that of James Wong, Peter Larson, and Edward Pentecost, published in 1973 as *Missions from the Third World.* Their survey showed 2,994 missionaries sent out by 212 agencies in 47 sending countries.[34]

Both the 1973 survey and more recent research by Lawrence Keyes and by Larry Pate reveal questions of definition and of interpretation that make comparisons difficult. Mission agencies differ in their concepts of "missionaries." Some counts include only those sent internationally. Others include all who minister cross-culturally, whether in their own lands or foreign lands. Actually many Asian missionaries sent to foreign lands have ministered among their own cultural group (overseas Koreans, or Chinese, or Japanese, for example). In listing "home" missionaries, many agencies do not indicate which ones are in cross-cultural ministry. Thus researchers must decide what persons to count, recognizing that their results must be interpreted with appropriate caution.

A 1980 survey by Lawrence Keyes was published as *The Last Age of Missions*.[35] He reported 10,841 missionaries from non-Western lands, sent out by 368 agencies. The remarkable increase from the report seven years earlier was due at least in part to more thorough research--but mission outreach from Asia, Africa, and Latin America was obviously growing quite rapidly.

Larry Pate, in research done in 1988 and published in 1989 (under the title *From All Peoples*),[36] identified gaps in the earlier report of Keyes, and therefore suggested revised figures for 1980: totals of 13,238 missionaries and 743 sending agencies.

For 1988, Pate reported 35,924 missionaries from 1,094 agencies in 118 countries! His revised figures for 1980 and his 1988 count should be comparable, with the same researcher and the same methodology. Thus the great increase (at an average rate of 13.3 percent per year) probably reflects an actual rapid expansion of Third World missionary forces--and a valuable new Christian resource for world evangelization. (It should be noted, however, that Pate indicates about 80 percent of the reported missionaries serve cross-culturally within their own nations.)

These surveys dealt only with Protestant and/or evangelical mission outreach. Comparable figures for AD 2000 have not been published. Pate and others estimated that the number of non-Western missionaries would exceed 50,000 by 2000.

The new *World Christian Encyclopedia* does include a category, country by country and with a world total, of "citizens sent" outside their own lands for Christian work. The figures do not include persons in cross-cultural work in their homelands. They do include representatives of all bodies claiming Christian faith--not just Protestants. The world total is given as 419,524. Of that number, 83,454 come from Latin America, Africa, and Asia. That portion of the world "missionary" force is 19.9 percent.

For several decades, representatives of cross-cultural mission societies in various non-Western lands have joined together in national organizations for mutual interaction. In 1989 a "Third World Missions Association" was formed to extend such mutual sharing and consultation to the global level. This is a further indicator of the increasing prominence of Third World leadership in world Christianity--a vital part of the shifting center of gravity of the Christian faith.

4

THEOLOGICAL CROSSCURRENTS

Developments in theology are a significant element in Christian history, with effects far beyond the academic or intellectual circles where they usually begin. Formal theology deals with analyses and statements of Christian doctrine. But informally it is a matter of personal convictions as the basis for lifestyle and relationships. What may begin as secluded and often abstract concepts can eventually mold the thoughts and lives of millions who are not theologically literate.

Expansion of Christianity--in numbers, spread, vitality, or influence--is inseparably related to its doctrinal foundation. Latourette pointed out that the clarity and the stamina of Christian faith at different times and places have been clearly reflected in the rapidity and extent of Christian advance.

In the closing decades of the 20th century, many theological movements have vied for acceptance. Their differing views have interacted with one another and with secular philosophies. Some theologies have a broad general following, while others have remained mostly in the realm of academic discussion. New and sometimes conflicting proposals have produced bewildering crosscurrents of religious ideas.

The Postmodern Paradigm

Underlying much theological thought and discussion in recent years is the ongoing secular shift from modern to postmodern assumptions. Principles associated with the Enlightenment, with the resultant emphasis on reason and science, were dominant in the Western world for about three centuries. David Bosch has analyzed at length the effects of that "modern" paradigm on Christian thought and practice. He stated that "on the whole, Catholic theology and the Catholic Church withstood Enlightenment influences more effectively than did Protestantism." For Protestantism, however, "virtually everything that happened since the eighteenth century was... profoundly influenced by the Enlightenment."[37]

As noted earlier (in the chapter on context), the West is experiencing gradual change in its basic philosophical assumptions. The emerging postmodern view has not entirely displaced emphasis on reason and science, but it does challenge accepted principles in many ways (Bosch again offers an extended analysis).[38]

During the ascendancy of the modern paradigm, Christianity and other religions had to face growing secularization of all of life. In 1928, an international Christian conference at Jerusalem urged all religions to combat together the threat of materialistic secularism. Though some recovery of religion was evident later, Christian theology also included tendencies toward accommodation with secularism (evident in the writings of Bonhoeffer, Hoekendijk, and Harvey Cox).

The rise of postmodernism, welcomed by some because it might reduce materialism and encourage spiritual concerns, led mainly to an amorphous spirituality that simply posed a new and different challenge to Christian faith.

The recent appearance of process theology and current controversy over the "openness" of God are perhaps only indirectly related to postmodern concepts. But they share with the new paradigm a principle of uncertainty in contrast to the relative fixedness of traditional theology. How widely such views will spread and how much influence they will have on Christian thought, and on the progress of the faith, remain to be seen.

Polarization and Moderation

At the beginning of the 1970s, emphases of Protestant Christians (primarily in the West, but to some extent worldwide) were polarized between social and evangelistic concerns. A long history and deeply-held doctrinal differences intensified the clash of positions and purposes.

Observers have identified the beginning of the division with what came to be called the "social gospel," starting early in the 20th century (led notably by Walter Rauschenbusch). What was initially intended only to strengthen social concerns, alongside the church's evangelistic mandate, was seen by some as a substitute for evangelism. Apparently some Christians, affected by theories based in Darwinian ideas or by radical biblical criticism, did not feel comfortable with traditional evangelism and gravitated toward social action instead.

By mid-century, the opposing emphases represented differing theologies, usually called "liberal" and "conservative." They had developed into separate camps, often identified as "conciliar" on the one hand (because of common affiliation with councils of churches) and "evangelical" on the other. Of course there was overlapping, since many with evangelical doctrinal positions were also members of churches involved in national or world councils of churches (such as John R. W. Stott, for example).

One camp defined Christian responsibility almost entirely in terms of working for a more just society, and for human welfare in general. Its program gave little place, and indeed little attention, to evangelism. The opposite camp so fixed its attention and its purposes on evangelism and missions that it often considered any social emphasis at best a distraction, and perhaps even a departure from right doctrine and Christian duty.

Papers prepared for an assembly of the World Council of Churches at Uppsala, Sweden, in 1968 sparked open controversy between proponents of the opposing views. The final Uppsala document was perceived as predominantly liberal in theology. In response to such statements, a group of "confession-minded" (conservative) German theologians produced in 1970 what is called the Frankfurt Declaration, giving voice to a clear and strong evangelical position.

An especially radical liberal position emerged from a 1972 conference at Bangkok, with the theme of "Salvation Today"--interpreted largely in terms of "humanization." Though the Commission on World Mission and Evangelism of the World Council of Churches sponsored the conference, it gave little attention to mission or evangelism as traditionally understood and practiced. A World Council assembly at Nairobi in 1975 gave evidence of some shifting back toward a less extreme position, plus also some affirmation of evangelization. (Donald McGavran gathered relevant documents and commentary in *The Conciliar-Evangelical Debate*, published in 1977.)[39] Later World Council conferences continued the trend toward a more balanced stance.

In the meantime, evangelicals gathered in a Congress on World Evangelization at Lausanne, Switzerland, in 1974 (at the initiative of Billy Graham). That conference, and the Lausanne Movement which it introduced, gave greater recognition to Christian social concerns than many evangelicals had given earlier. In fact, a vocal evangelical minority both then and more recently have strongly advocated more holistic ministries, complementing evangelism with emphasis on a wide range of human needs.[40]

This controversy within Western Christianity has been especially relevant to the spread and strength of the faith. Many theological questions may not affect expansion directly, either positively or negatively. But this polarization pertained specifically to the purpose and the mission of the church.

By the century's end, the polarity of liberal and conservative theologies, of identifiable conciliar and evangelical positions, and of primary emphasis on social or on spiritual concerns had by no means disappeared. But positions were not as one-sided as they had been in mid-century. And controversy between adherents of the two positions had moderated. Most Western Christians were ready to agree on the importance of holistic ministry, uniting evangelistic witness and social ministries.

As noted above, this dichotomy was confined largely to the West. There were echoes in other parts of the world, but Christians in Latin America, Asia, and Africa tended to be strongly evangelical and at the same time gave much emphasis to social ministries.

Outflow from Vatican II

The Roman Catholic Church also has experienced theological struggle in the late 20th century--much of it in assimilating and interpreting positions established through the ecumenical council known as Vatican II (1962-1965). It has proved to be a watershed in Catholic thought.

For almost a century prior to Vatican II, Catholicism seemed to be a closed system, staunchly defending itself against the modern world. The original Vatican Council of 1869-1870 had staked out strong dogmatic positions against the "liberalism" of Western society. There was little or no interaction with Protestantism.

"Against this background," as David Bosch observed, "the events of Vatican II were little short of a miracle. A new spirit permeated virtually all the proceedings and documents of the Council."[41] It is reported that Pope John XXIII had wanted to "let some fresh air into the church!"[42] In that, he obviously succeeded.

Vatican II introduced a turnaround in many aspects of the Roman Church's posture--with new openness, new tolerance, new readiness to cooperate with Protestants and with others. The Church expanded its emphasis on the laity, on the Bible, and on use of vernacular languages in worship. A minor reform, but symbolic of changed attitudes, was increased freedom for monks and nuns to wear everyday clothing.

The radically altered approaches from Vatican II began to spread through the Church worldwide--though not all at once. The process was gradual, mixed, and incomplete. It was much more rapid in some regions than in others. For example, when Catholics and Protestants were already working together in many ways in North America, some Catholic priests in Latin America were still involved in persecution of evangelical Christians. But by 1970, the outflow of a new spirit, vision, and doctrinal stance was well under way.

Reappraisal of other religions (as well as of Protestantism) was a major element in the work of Vatican II. Robert J. Schreiter has appraised that change, suggesting that "shifts in theological thinking during the Council brought about a 'period of missionary crisis'" in the Church.[43] He identified the crisis as continuing until 1975, as Catholic interpreters sought to "consolidate... implications suggested by the positions taken during the Council." In reviewing various Church documents on into the 1980s, he cited a concluding statement of a 1981 seminar as "the charter of the contemporary missionary movement in the Catholic Church"--with its "fourfold emphasis on proclamation, dialogue, inculturation, and liberation."

Toward the close of the century, the Catholic Church was still struggling with various doctrinal questions, such as the role of women, clerical celibacy, abortion and birth control, and the place of the Virgin Mary in traditional theology. Vatican II had provided no clear guidance toward resolution of these issues.

Religious Relativism

The Roman Church has not been alone in reassessing other religions, to arrive at a theological understanding of their existence and their nature, and of their relation to the Christian faith. Protestants also have struggled to develop a "theology of religions" (identified by David Bosch as a new formal branch of theology which has "evolved only since the 1960s").[44]

As the world has become more cosmopolitan, with religions in much closer contact everywhere, the obvious plurality of religions has produced a "pluralism" that accepts the reality of the many faiths and seeks ways to interpret them and relate to them. Such questions have become a prominent theme in theological literature. The result has been what Bosch calls a "bewildering diversity" of interpretations. One scholar has listed and classified 27 differing theologies of religion. Most, though, can be grouped as subtypes under a few main categories. Bosch calls the main views exclusivism, fulfillment, and relativism.[45]

Enlightenment views that had prevailed during the long dominance of the modern paradigm were conducive to relativism, since matters of faith did not lend themselves to scientific proof. The emerging postmodern paradigm is especially friendly to relativism. It is increasingly skeptical of any objective truth and holds tolerance (often merging into indifference) as a prime value. Western society, "given its understanding of tolerance based in relativism, finds the question of exclusiveness to be a stumbling block and a scandal."[46]

The dominant trend in writing on religions during the past three decades has been relativist. Prominent Catholic theologians (such as Karl Rahner and H. R. Schlette) have spoken of devoted followers of other faiths as "anonymous Christians," with those faiths being for them the "ordinary ways of salvation." John Hick, an outstanding Protestant writer on religions, has promoted a "Copernican revolution" by which Christians would not focus on Christ, but on God. Wilfred Cantwell Smith made sincerity of faith (rather than the object of faith) the basis of salvation.

Relativism has not had the field of theological discourse entirely to itself. Many theologians of orthodox or conservative views, and even more evangelicals, with generous appreciation for the values of other religions, have still maintained that Jesus and the Christian message are unique, and that the "salvation" sought by other religions is often quite different from that offered in Christ. Lesslie Newbigin is an outstanding representative of this position (as Hendrik Kraemer had been in earlier decades).

For several decades, dialogue between adherents of different faiths has been a noteworthy Christian emphasis . It has had special popularity among those with relativist views, but its value has been recognized as well by conservatives and evangelicals (such as John R. W. Stott).

Relativists have sometimes proposed dialogue as a substitute for witness (which they have thought undesirable because it would usually see conversion as a desired outcome). But a more common Christian view has considered dialogue as an appropriate expression of Christian friendliness and openness, most often accompanied by witness. In that connection, Bosch cites a 1979 World Council of Churches document that describes dialogue as "witnessing to our deepest convictions, while listening to those of our neighbors."[47] True dialogue assumes that both parties to the discussion will share their own faith freely, and that they will learn from each other, without compromising their own faith.

Liberation Theology

Already noted as an indication of the shifting Christian center of gravity, liberation theology has brought a fresh current into recent Christian thought and discussion. Its central vision and main themes developed in the 1960s among Roman Catholics in Latin America. The term "liberation theology" was first used in 1968.

Observers have judged the new religious climate created by Pope John XXIII and Vatican II to be the nurturing environment for liberation views,[48] and disillusionment with "development" as the pivotal cause.[49] Founders of the movement saw development efforts as too slow and ineffective to remedy the injustices and the resulting poverty of their condition. Radical change--liberation, or revolution--would be necessary. Their purpose was to provide spiritual foundations that could inspire oppressed people to take action for socio-economic transformation.

Though in some respects suggestive of classical theological liberalism, which for the better part of a century had emphasized social issues and systemic change, liberation theology originated independently, and from a very different base. It is a prime example of contextualized theology, grounded in what its adherents call "praxis," or experience. It is theology "from below," rising from depressed and marginalized segments of society. As such, it found ready response from other Christians (both Catholic and Protestant) in similar circumstances.

Liberation theology has found its central biblical motif in the Exodus. It has focused also on many other Bible teachings that touch on deliverance, especially from oppression or poverty, noting that traditional interpretations have often tended to spiritualize such passages.

God's "preferential option for the poor" has been an emerging Roman Catholic doctrinal emphasis, loosely akin to the concerns of the liberation movement. The Catholic Church first affirmed it in 1968, just as the liberation theme was beginning to gain prominence, and it has been widely accepted and supported, with recognition from Protestants also.

Liberation theology has been controversial, for two main reasons: its Bible interpretations have been judged to be seriously flawed, based on eisegesis rather than exegesis; and several of its proponents have relied heavily on Marxist economic theories. More recently liberation views have tended to shy away from these problems and come closer to orthodox (and sometimes even evangelical) positions.

Influence of liberation theology has spread widely--far more than any other Third World theology. It has sparked the formation of what Art Glasser has called "a proliferation of liberation theologies," reflecting the conditions of many other people groups who feel themselves to be oppressed and in need of liberation.[50] Furthermore, the movement has impelled theologians of all schools to include greater attention to poverty, oppression, and deliverance in their own doctrinal schemes.

Other Theological Emphases

The closing decades of the 20th century intensified a focus on eschatology which began earlier in the century. David Bosch, after citing a statement of Ernst Troeltsch about 19th century Christian theology, that "the eschatology office is mostly closed," followed then by saying, "In our century the 'eschatology office' has been working overtime."[51] He used that contrast to lead into a chapter on "Mission as Action in Hope."

Under the discouraging impact of two world wars, and especially in continental Europe, theologians gave renewed attention to eschatology. A German theologian, Jurgen Moltmann, published in 1967 his *Theology of Hope* and followed up in 1975 with *The Experiment Hope*. Eschatology is the theological expression of Christian hope. Interest in and further discussion of the theology of hope, and of eschatology in general, spread widely in Western church and theological circles.

On a more popular level, the approach of the year 2000 augmented public interest in the future. A small minority among premillennialists suggested that Christ would return to earth at that time. Though not speculating as to the exact timing of Christ's return, a large segment of conservative Christians did immerse themselves in study of Bible prophecy and did proclaim that His return seemed near. Hal Lindsey's book, *The Late Great Planet Earth,*[52] stimulated a stream of books and films dealing with expected events of the "last days," which in turn produced a vigorous revival of premillennialist views. Meanwhile, Christians of many doctrinal views were multiplying their efforts at world evangelization, using AD 2000 as a target date--and hoping thereby to hasten the Lord's return.

In many places where Christians were undergoing suffering and perhaps martyrdom, "the last things" had never ceased to be of vital importance. But renewed interest in eschatology in the Western world made it a worldwide concern by the close of the millennium.

The kingdom of God was another cardinal theological motif of the past thirty years. It rose to some degree from the focus on eschatology, since there are biblical links between the return of the Lord and the coming of the kingdom. A concept of the kingdom as "already--but not yet" tied it to past and present, but also to the future, and to the remaining mission of the church.

The World Council of Churches made God's kingdom the overall theme for its worldwide assembly in 1980 at Melbourne. That was an outstanding symbolic expression of the range and depth of the kingdom emphasis in current Christianity.

In recent years it has become commonplace to relate the kingdom of God essentially to the mission of the church. Johannes Verkuyl in 1978, in *Contemporary Missiology*, stated the kingdom as the ultimate goal of the *missio Dei*. Orlando Costas in 1982, in *Christ Outside the Gate: Mission Beyond Christendom*, treated the kingdom as the "frame of reference" for mission. Art Glasser in 1983, in *Contemporary Theologies of Mission*, made the kingdom of God his unifying theme for a chapter on "The Whole-Bible Basis of Mission,"[53]

Biblical references to the kingdom of God can be understood and interpreted in many different ways. There is no unanimity of views as to the nature of the kingdom, its relationship to the people of God and to society in general, its connection with the church, or its expected future. But such questions have become a much larger part of Christian thought and discussion than was true until fairly recent decades.

5

MISSIOLOGY

Ever since the days of William Carey and other pioneers of modern missions (from 1792), throughout what Latourette identified as the "great century" of Christian expansion (1815-1914), and on up to the present, intentional mission outreach has been a crucial factor in Christian spread and growth.

Organized study of the premises and the processes involved in mission outreach was slow in developing, and even slower in gaining recognition as an academic discipline.[54] Such study was given various names, such as theory of missions, science of missions, or missions principles and practice. By the last half of the 20th century, "missiology" became the common term. It is a very broad field, including biblical, theological, historical, and strategic elements--and related to most aspects of human life (anthropological, cultural, economic, political, social, etc.). Its scope is worldwide. It deals explicitly with the frontiers of Christian faith, in direct contact with the non-Christian world, which are most critical for spread and growth.

As modern missions evolved from less self-conscious beginnings to formal analysis and careful planning today, missiological insights, movements and emphases have played an ever increasing part in Christian spread and growth. These developments have had their main *locus* in the Western World (and most prominently in America)--but their influence has spread to other regions, often through international conferences, and most notably as non-Western mission agencies have multiplied.

Research and Strategy

Formation of the International Association for Mission Studies in 1972 and then the American Society of Missiology in 1973 reflect both the maturing of missiology as a field of study, and a growing interest in research and in strategy planning in missions. The American Society of Missiology publishes the quarterly journal, *Missiology.* The *International Review of Mission* had been published already for many years by the International Missionary Council, and then after 1960 by the Commission on World Mission and Evangelism of the World Council of Churches. Other scholarly journals on missions arose in various parts of the world to engage in missiological thought and discussion.

David Barrett's contribution to missions research has been and is outstanding. He began with research on Christianity in Africa, especially the continent's independent Christian movements. Asked then to prepare a new edition of the *World Christian Handbook* (a small survey published at intervals before 1970), he spent almost twelve years, including visits to more than 100 nations, to produce the amazingly comprehensive *World Christian Encyclopedia* (published in 1982). The even more extensive, two-volume update edition came out early this year. Barrett is widely recognized by all Christian groups as the most prominent current authority on the status of world Christianity.

Modern technology has made possible the detailed work of Barrett and other researchers. Exhaustive computer data bases now contain information about almost every aspect of religions around the world, along with their secular contexts. Various Christian organizations have produced data bases to meet their own planning needs--and in the past decade, sharing of data between agencies has become commonplace.

A veritable mountain of books on missiological themes has come from the presses in recent decades--and the pace still quickens. Most concentrate on one particular concern relevant to the Christian mission, but some are more general in nature (such as Verkuyl's *Contemporary Missiology* in 1978), or more specifically directed toward actual planning processes (such as Dayton and Fraser's *Planning Strategies for World Evangelization* in 1980).[55]

Missiological research and writing have been supplemented by conferences far too numerous to recount. Some focused especially on missions *per se* (including a consultation in 1974 on the future of the missionary enterprise and another in 1982 on the role of Western missionaries in today's world). Of a more general nature, but with much greater overall influence on the Christian faith worldwide, was the International Congress on World Evangelization at Lausanne, Switzerland, in 1974, with the ongoing movement it sponsored.

Missions agencies which had done their planning for years (or even for generations) without much awareness of "strategy," began by the 1970s to produce formal schemes for planning and formal mission statements and strategy documents. Much of this change occurred under the influence of modern Western business methods, with their emphasis on "management by objectives" or r similar approaches. Gradually these ideas spread to other parts of the world, where informal and intuitive ways had been culturally more comfortable, often causing tensions among Third World Christians who had ambivalent feelings about Western ways.

The field of missiology, quite naturally, has produced persons known as missiologists--those devoting themselves to the study and interpretation of the Christian mission, and especially its principles and strategy. These have been the thinkers and writers who have produced the books on missions, taught with that specialization, conducted missions conferences, and led in the planning of church and missions agencies. Their influence on the spread and growth of the Christian faith in recent years has been significant. A few of the most outstanding missiologists have been influential enough to affect the purposes and the emphases of a large segment of the Christian movement.

Church Growth

For about a century, by far the most influential missiological motif was the "three-self" pattern proposed in the mid-1800s by Rufus Anderson and Henry Venn--that churches arising in mission fields should become self-propagating, self-governing, and self-supporting. Roland Allen in the early 20th century gave that indigenous ideal strong support, as did a wide range of missions agencies, consultations and publications in succeeding decades.

By 1970, Donald McGavran's church growth principles had taken center stage in discussion and writing about missions. For about twenty years, from the publishing in 1955 of his seminal book, *The Bridges of God,*[56] until the middle or late 1970s, McGavran was the world's most prominent and influential missiologist.

McGavran's views reflected a background of childhood in India and 31 years as a missionary there. Convinced that his insights would have relevance far beyond India, he left for America to promote them through writing, teaching, and speaking. He sought to blend his ideas into a coherent strategy, as reflected in his book's subtitle, "A Study in the Strategy of Missions." He explained it further in his 1959 sequel, *How Churches Grow*, and his definitive work, *Understanding Church Growth*, in 1970.[57]

With the rapid spread of interest in McGavran's church growth principles, others soon joined him in what became a full-fledged movement. His Institute of Church Growth was adopted by Fuller Theological Seminary and became its School of World Mission, which attracted students from many lands. Before long the movement gave birth to a church growth periodical, a book club, and a publishing house with special interest in church growth material.

From the beginning, McGavran was concerned primarily for rapid evangelization of potentially responsive people groups around the world. To encourage that, he emphasized research and strategic planning, the primacy of evangelism in mission work, focus on those people groups that are most responsive, and cultural adaptation. McGavran hoped that these and other related principles might be applied to Christian outreach worldwide--and many missionaries and non-Western Christian leaders began using these approaches in their work.

In 1972, McGavran and a colleague, Peter Wagner, turned toward America (and also, by implication, other parts of the Western world), to see how the movement's concepts might accelerate Christian growth in long-established work.

Though several of McGavran's proposed principles proved to be controversial, even that was also evidence of the extent of his influence. Judging from the profusion of books, articles, reports, conferences, and discussions it inspired, church growth must be appraised as the chief missiological emphasis of the 1960s and 1970s. Though exact measurement is impossible, there is no doubt that the movement contributed largely to more rapid spread of Christian faith in those decades.

Unreached Peoples

Since 1970, attention of the Christian mission enterprise has focused increasingly on people groups, rather than on nations. To be sure, tribal societies (such as those in much of Africa) had been approached earlier as separate ethnic and cultural groups. Some independent missions agencies had focused their efforts on tribal peoples. Cameron Townsend in 1942 formed the Wycliffe Bible Translators to provide scriptures for additional ethno-linguistic groups. But the main thrust of Christian missions still largely addressed nations, not peoples.

Donald McGavran was the prime mover in a change of focus by giving central attention (in *The Bridges of God*) to people movements, and by raising the question, "How do peoples become Christians?" In 1959, in *How Churches Grow*, he pointed out that a nation is often a "conglomerate" of many peoples, rather than a homogeneous whole. ("Mosaic" later became the more favored term.) That point of view gradually infused missiological thought.

The Lausanne International Congress on World Evangelization in 1974 proved crucial in bringing people groups to the forefront of Christian attention. Conference planners asked researchers to prepare a directory listing about 450 "unreached" peoples (those mostly without the gospel). Ralph Winter, a colleague of McGavran at Fuller Seminary, then gave a major address on the unreached peoples.

Winter left the faculty of the School of World Missions at Fuller Seminary in 1976 to form his own organization, the U.S. Center for World Mission, expressly to promote a new missiological challenge: work among all the remaining unevangelized peoples. By aggressive leadership through publications and conferences, he succeeded in turning much of the evangelical mission movement to this new emphasis. In 1980, Winter brought together at Edinburgh a World Consultation on Frontier Missions, with its theme of "A Church for Every People by the Year 2000."[58]

This refocusing of the aims of mission agencies has called for consultation to define unreached peoples and to agree on terminology, and then research to identify the unreached peoples. Winter put the current emphasis in historical context in reference to earlier eras of modern missions, which concentrated first on coastland areas, and then on continental interiors, but bypassed many people groups in the process. He also pointed out the large population blocs (in China, India, and the Muslim world) that dominate the remaining task of world evangelization.

Winter effectively shifted the main theme of today's missiology from church growth to unreached peoples, thereby becoming the most influential missiologist of the 1980s and 1990s. It is interesting that McGavran first directed Christian attention to people groups, as a lead-in to his concern for growth; and that he and Winter were colleagues at Fuller--but their strategy thrusts move in opposite directions. McGavran wanted major effort to concentrate on responsive peoples, where the harvest is ripe, but Winter urges concentration on places where the gospel seed has not yet been sown. (Most missions agencies, meanwhile, have taken a both-and approach, rather than doctrinaire adherence to any one missiological scheme.)

By the mid-1980s, the approaching end of the century (and the millennium) had stimulated other forces to augment the push to reach all people groups. David Barrett, through his research and correspondence, became aware of up to 200 mission agencies (denominational or independent) with special plans for accelerated evangelization, about half of them using AD 2000 as a target date. Since no human effort had incited this common thrust, it seemed clear evidence of widespread moving of God's Spirit, stirring up a Global Evangelization Movement.

In support of the movement, a series of books (the AD 2000 Series) was produced, to provide background material. Barrett himself prepared several of the books. He and his associates also began a quarterly trends newsletter, the *AD 2000 Global Monitor*. Aware of common purposes, mission agencies began networking, sharing plans and research data and prayer concerns.

In 1989 at Singapore, more then 300 persons from more than 50 countries and many mission agencies met to consider the missions task for the remainder of the century. David Barrett prepared carefully researched documents for their study. An ongoing organization, the AD 2000 Movement, developed from that conference--giving concentrated attention to plans for evangelizing peoples who have little access to the gospel.[59] It changed its name later to the AD 2000 and Beyond Movement, and initiated the Joshua Project to focus on the most urgent of the unreached peoples.

Barrett used his own formula to portray the unevangelized portion of the world, calling it World A, in contrast with World C (the Christian part) and world B (non-Christian but already evangelized). By his own estimate, even as late as AD 2000, World A included 26.9 percent of the world's people (down from 44.4 percent in 1970). He and others produced reports and maps to popularize the concept and arouse concern for the remaining task of evangelization. Barrett pointed out that the vast majority of Christian missionaries work in World B, or even World C, and only a tiny fraction of funding for missions is used for World A. He challenged mission agencies to review their strategy, asking what countries or peoples may most need missionaries.

To emphasize the same concern, the AD 2000 Movement used a different formula: the "10-40 window." It represented the vast area between 10 and 40 north latitudes, extending from western Africa across the Middle East and southern and southeastern Asia--where the great majority of unreached peoples live. Thus the two schemes describe the same need in slightly different ways. Both have been useful to Christians in pointing a direction for Christian mission.

A more recent emphasis has called not just for an initial Christian impact within each people group, but rather for stimulating an ongoing "church planting movement within every people."[60]

As with the church growth movement, so also the emphasis on unreached peoples has undoubtedly contributed largely to spread and growth of the Christian faith in recent years.

Contextualization

For some years before 1970, many missiologists had pointed out a deficiency in the traditional "three-self" formula used to measure indigenous church strength. It failed to address the important matter of relating gospel and church to local culture. Thus new mission work might meet all the expected criteria but be entirely foreign in nature, without roots in the real soil of its environment.

To stress cultural relevance in Christian missions, the term "contextualization" came into increasingly common use from 1972. Its central question is the relationship of Christian faith to local culture. The term itself has applied most notably to the search for culturally appropriate theologies, but its scope is much broader, touching all aspects of evangelism and Christian life. The issues involved are complex and sensitive, with the danger of Christianity so foreign as to be practically irrelevant (at one extreme), or so distorted by syncretism as to lose its essence (at the other extreme). What valid contextualization seeks is a balance of biblical truth and cultural relevance.[61]

Though the term is relatively new, the Christian faith really has been adapting to its various contexts from the beginning--often without awareness of the process or of cultural realities. The New Testament reflects the struggle to contextualize in the Greco-Roman world. What has been relatively new in the past thirty years is a veritable flood of books, articles, and conferences examining the church and culture.

The Consultation on Gospel and Culture, sponsored by the Lausanne Movement in 1978, had special significance, in its Willowbank Report providing an excellent summary of the concerns and the principles involved in contextualization.[62]

As a result of this new emphasis, missiology has given increasing attention to cultural anthropology. This, along with the current focus on people groups, has fit in well with recent secular trends emphasizing ethnicity. Aboriginal populations in modern highly developed nations, for example, have gained new visibility. Their cultures are now being valued, rather than denigrated.

The intentional effort to make Christian faith more at home within various cultures clearly facilitates the spread of the gospel. It enables persons in all kinds of settings to understand the message and respond to it without having to change worldviews and thought patterns as a condition for being Christian. As with other missiological principles, it has been easier to state the ideal and give it formal endorsement than to turn the intention into reality--but contextualization is increasingly evident in world Christianity.

Holistic Missions

What has in recent decades been called holistic missions--a blend of witness and ministry, of word and deed--is nothing new. As in the case of adaptation to culture, it has been intrinsic to the Christian faith from the beginning. Jesus ministered to all kinds of needs, and so did the early apostles.

Conditions both external and internal to the faith have, from time to time, hindered one side or the other of the church's expression of its mission. As noted earlier, much of the 20th century saw a polarization in which one segment of Western Christianity stressed evangelism and neglected social ministries, while another segment stressed such ministries and downplayed evangelism. As further noted, that cleavage showed evidence of healing toward the century's end.

Since 1970, missiology has intensified the emphasis on holism. As in the case of contextualization, that increased intensity has produced an expanding literature. It has also multiplied the varieties of Christian care for human needs. Educational and medical work have characterized modern missions from the first: William Carey, the noted missions pioneer, was accompanied by both types of ministry. But in recent decades, as emerging nations have assumed increasing responsibility for meeting health and educational needs of their people, Christians have expanded their ministries in many new directions.

Development is a major concern in most less industrialized lands. International financial organizations and governments of more prosperous nations have provided grants and/or loans for projects in Third World countries. Many non-government organizations (NGOs), including Christian denominations and independent Christian agencies, have provided aid also. The range of types of projects has been quite broad (such as public health, agriculture, well-drilling, housing, job training, handicraft enterprises).

Disaster relief has become a much larger part of Christian ministry in the past thirty years. Drought and famine in the Sahel region of Africa in the 1970s stimulated greatly increased concern for world hunger. Wars, earthquakes, floods, hurricanes, volcanic eruptions--all kinds of disasters brought outpourings of relief funds and the sending of relief teams to disaster areas.

Another, though less common, expression of Christian holistic aims has been action for social change (as, for example, in resistance to *apartheid* in South Africa).

In these development activities, Christians have been deeply involved with social and economic needs all across the world, and have related cooperatively with various non-Christian agencies engaged in similar projects. Such involvement helps create an atmosphere hospitable to Christian faith and often becomes an occasion for sharing of faith.

Non-Traditional Missions

The face of Christian missions has changed greatly, and in many ways, in recent decades. Note has been taken already of the rapid growth of missions from non-Western sources, and of several new directions and emphases in current missiology.

In earlier generations, Christian missions usually fit a fairly well defined and traditional pattern. Theologically trained persons from Western lands went to "mission fields" in other parts of the world for evangelism and church planting. Alongside such preacher missionaries, there were often also teachers, doctors, and nurses for educational and medical ministries. They went out as "career" missionaries, with long-range commitment to their tasks. They were sent to the field by missions societies (orders in the case of Roman Catholics) or denominational agencies that had clearly spiritual and church-oriented aims.

That picture was already beginning to change in the 1950s and 1960s, but most of the radical change has come since 1970. New political and economic conditions, new technologies, the post-modern psychology, and changing theological and missiological emphases have led to various innovations in missions.

An obvious shift has multiplied involvement of short-term personnel--some for periods of a few years, but thousands for brief projects of perhaps a week or two. Many new mission organizations have been set up specifically for short-range involvement. A few mission agencies which historically had only long-term missionaries now appoint persons only for an initial trial term of several years (partly in response to a society less inclined toward long-range commitments). The very brief projects are made possible, of course, by today's air travel and by the relative affluence of Western society.

In today's mobile world, millions of Christians live outside their homelands for extended time periods. They can help in sharing the gospel. Some Christian agencies have formalized this potential in programs called "tentmaking" (based on a practice of the apostle Paul as reported in Acts 18).
Many para-church organizations today play no part in direct evangelism or church planting, but assist in Christian ministries in supportive ways (such as development projects, logistics, or production of materials).

There has been a kind of "secularization" of mission personnel. It can no longer be assumed that most missionaries will be preachers with church-planting roles. Areas where Christian work is more mature have their own local evangelists and pastors. Therefore missionaries are more likely to be specialists. Almost all who participate in brief projects do so as specialists of some kind.

In most parts of the world, formal or traditional mission outreach is no longer the only or perhaps even the major way the Christian faith is extended. A fair number of countries and cultures do not welcome missionaries from outside. In a smaller number of lands, even insiders find freedom for open witness severely limited. In such places (sometimes called "closed" areas), believers may have many opportunities for service, and through that service to witness to their faith. The People's Republic of China, for instance, has not admitted missionaries, but has welcomed "foreign experts" to teach or provide other services to its people.

One non-traditional approach to unreached peoples has sought to elicit prayer and resources for focus on a particular people group by networking, to combine the concern and efforts of various Christian groups. The leader for such a network was called a "non-residential missionary"--though that title is now outdated, and "strategy coordinator" is the more common term. This plan and others developed for so-called closed countries have been called ways of "creative access." A most obvious and most common form of such access is broadcasting, often through one of the major outlets for international Christian radio.

Relationships

Indigenous principles in missions call for transfer of leadership (from outsiders who have initiated work to local believers), as soon as that transfer is feasible. But the process is not automatic, and both psychological and cultural factors often interfere. Thus questions of relationships in missions have been a major concern from the beginning of the modern missions era.

A 1971 conference on "Missions in Creative Tension" examined thoroughly the structural and practical issues encountered by missionaries from outside and indigenous Christians in the everyday experiences of working together.[63]

In the early 1970s, some African church leaders issued a call for "moratorium"--temporary withdrawal of European and American missionaries--in order to allow Africans to give full guidance to the life and work of Africa's churches. The proposal itself never gained wide backing, but it did focus attention on delay in transfer of responsibility, and thus helped to move the process forward.

More recently there has been growing internationalization of missionary forces--with missionary teams made up of persons from various countries. This both helps relationships (by diluting the earlier division into two opposing sides) and complicates them (by bringing more different cultures into the mix).

At the same time, mission agencies have been drawing closer to each other, as noted earlier, in the process called "networking." This includes sharing of information (such as computerized data bases), plans, and prayer concerns--and agreements to work together on various projects.

Relationships among Christians and Christian workers have a tremendous impact, for good or for harm, on the spread of the faith. Problems that loomed so large a generation ago have faded from prominence with increased attention to unreached peoples. Relationships often are better in working toward a common purpose that in merely talking about relationships. Thus any possible hindrance to the gospel from poor relationships has diminished.

Closure

Toward the end of the century, some evangelical speakers and writers began to anticipate "closure"--the completion of the mission task. A few related their expectation to the year 2000, as a possible time for Christ's return. Most simply spoke of this as "the last generation of missionaries," or wrote of "bringing back the King" by fulfilling our mission responsibility. Some referred to "completing the Great Commission."[64] Even those promoting the idea failed to agree on just what they meant by it, or on other relevant terminology.

The most common approach to closure has been linked to a popular understanding of Matthew 24:14. The verse speaks of the gospel being proclaimed "as a testimony to all nations," adding "and then the end will come" (NIV). The urgent mission advance related to the Global Evangelization Movement in the final quarter of the century and the hope for "A Church for Every People by the Year 2000" gave great encouragement to the idea. Advocates of reaching every people group with the gospel often understand the Bible as indicating that is the remaining condition for the Lord's return. Other Christians, however, see serious theological problems in that conclusion, and find other reasonable interpretations of the Scripture passage.

In any event, the desire for fulfillment of God's purpose has added impetus to Christian mission efforts, and thus no doubt accelerated the spread of the gospel and extension of the church.

6

EXPRESSIONS OF VITALITY

One of Latourette's criteria for evaluating advance or decline in the strength of Christianity was signs of unusual energy. Vigor could be expressed in many ways. Latourette examined how the faith spread, with special attention to fresh forms of witness and of outreach. When little new was happening, he took that as an indicator of spiritual weakness; but many new initiatives, giving rise to new organizations and new forms of ministry, he saw as evidence of growth in the spiritual power of the faith.

The Type that Is Spreading

In analyzing progress within a specific time frame, Latourette noted that segments of Christianity did not all advance at the same rate. He always asked what types of Christianity were most dramatically spreading and flourishing. Those types seemed to have the most vitality, whereas other types might be relatively quiescent (for a variety of reasons, both external and internal).

In the past thirty years, as we have noted, the Christian faith as a whole has been spreading and growing impressively. Some portions do seem indeed to be fairly quiescent or even declining (such as the established state churches of western Europe, with a net decrease in membership and little evidence of new outreach). But realistic evaluation sees renewal in eastern Europe and outstanding progress in Africa and Asia as outweighing any nominal losses for the Christian faith in western Europe.

The evangelical portion of Christianity, with its emphasis on proclamation of the gospel and on the necessity for a personal faith commitment to Christ, has increased more rapidly than Christianity as a whole. As noted earlier, David Barrett has reported evangelical growth between 1970 and 2000 from 2.5 percent of world population to 3.5 percent. His broader category of "Great Commission Christians" (dedicated to gospel outreach to the whole world) have grown from 7.5 percent to 10.7 percent during the same period. These groups hold with tenacity, and often with enthusiasm, beliefs that motivate them to strive for growth and spread of the faith.

What is broadly known as the charismatic movement has shown especially dramatic growth. Already by 1970 it was expanding quite rapidly, as Peter Wagner noted in his 1973 book, *Look Out! The Pentecostals Are Coming.*[65] David Barrett uses the combined term "Pentecostals/Charismatics" to encompass "three waves of renewal," all emphasizing the work of the Holy Spirit and personal charismatic experience.[66] He has identified the three waves as Pentecostal, charismatic, and neocharismatic. By now they exist in all branches of Christendom (not just in separate Pentecostal denominations).

Barrett showed Pentecostals and charismatics as 2.0 percent of world population in 1970, and 8.7 percent by AD 2000--by now a remarkable 27.7 percent of "organized global Christianity."[67]

In areas of the Western world where traditional Protestants, and especially the established churches, are stagnant or declining, there are types of Christianity showing vitality. In eastern Europe, the Orthodox churches have been revived following the breakup of Communism, and Pentecostals have been growing in western Europe. In Latin America, the dominant Roman Catholic Church has not kept pace with population growth; but Protestants and independents, and especially Pentecostals, have prospered. In North America, both Pentecostals and independent evangelicals have grown faster than population.

The African independent churches, which had separated from Western mission origins, or had originated *de novo* apart from any mission connections, are continuing to thrive and spread. Their practices generally include charismatic elements.

The church in China, as described in detail in an earlier chapter, has had unusually spectacular growth. Since 1949 it has been separated from its roots in the Western missionary movement. Under communism, it has become post-denominational (except for a continuing distinction between Protestant and Catholic). It is largely dependent on lay leadership, especially in the quite numerous unregistered congregations. The Chinese church is warmly evangelical and in a considerable measure charismatic. In many respects it parallels the traits of those segments of the faith that are growing and spreading elsewhere.

From Christian advance in such disparate circumstances, we see clearly that the type of Christianity that grows in today's world is confident in its beliefs, deeply committed, often enthusiastic about sharing the faith with others. Nominal Christianity shows only demographic growth (excess of births over deaths), if any at all.

Fresh Movements and Organizations

Latourette paid particular attention to the forming and expansion of new Christian enterprises. With the faith expanding so rapidly into more countries and among more peoples, that in itself has led to many fresh ventures and related structures, both in lands from which outreach originated, and in newly evolving Christian areas.

The Global Evangelization Movement (described already earlier) consisted of about 200 plans for expanded Christian outreach in the final quarter of the 20th century. It became linked to the missiological emphasis on unreached peoples. Together they motivated especially evangelicals, but also many other Christians, to accelerate gospel outreach looking toward AD 2000. In the process, they gave rise to various planning conferences, new organizations, and many publications (both periodicals and books), plus networking arrangements between agencies formerly in little contact with each other.

The Lausanne Movement, flowing from the 1974 international congress on evangelization at Lausanne, Switzerland, became an entirely new stream of cooperative endeavor involving Protestant and evangelical leaders. This was a new form of ecumenism, based on a shared aim to evangelize the world.

Other ecumenical structures continued, but without so much innovation. A major traditional thrust of what has been called the ecumenical movement, to encourage and initiate church unions, seemed to have stalled. David Barrett, in fact, in analyzing trends in the Christian world mission, has referred to several evident "failures" of the "drive for union." In contrast, he has noted rapid multiplying of new Christian denominations, estimating their rate of formation as nearly one a day.[68]

Most of the new entities may have arisen as Christianity found a foothold in additional nations or people groups. But a fair number likely came as offshoots from existing denominations (or churches)--and not just among Protestants. Barrett has pointedly named Orthodox and Anglican examples as well, and some new groups have separated from Roman Catholicism.

Fundamentalist movements have characterized recent decades--in Christianity as also in other religions. These have stated their purpose as recovery of basic religious truths, over against the doctrinal liberalism generated by modern and now postmodern cultures. Their strength comes partly from an emotional need for a secure foundation in a time of rapid change and uncertainties.

In many places (including, for example, Seoul and Singapore and Lagos, as well as American cities) what are called "mega-churches" have developed their own far-reaching mission programs. They often act independently, functioning for all practical purposes as mission agencies.

Expanded Resources and Ministries

A further expression of spiritual life and power in the Christian movement is rapid augmenting of resources made available to the movement and of ministries undertaken. Increase would be expected, simply from growth in the number of Christians--but the past thirty years have far exceeded expectations.

The number of Christians in the world grew by 61.7 percent

between 1970 and 2000. David Barrett gives figures for many aspects of Christian work in those years, enabling us to see how resources and ministries compare to numerical increase.[69]

Christian workers (personnel specifically devoted to Christian ministries) have more than doubled in the last three decades, for an annual growth rate more than 50 percent higher than the membership rate. Persons serving in foreign missions have increased only slightly more than membership, but the number of missions sending agencies has more than doubled (probably largely through the multiplying of non-Western agencies).

Religious broadcasting has developed rapidly, with Christian stations more than tripled (up 225 percent) and viewers/listeners almost tripled (up 186 percent). Barrett's tables do not show films, such as the *Jesus* film that has been shown worldwide.

Barrett gives exceptional emphasis to the amazing increase in the use of computers by Christians--a valuable resource now available, though surely even yet not fully utilized for spiritual purposes. He assumes only a thousand computers in Christian use in 1970, and 400 million today!

Barrett's report on financial resources for Christian causes is much less encouraging. Though the dollar amount for AD 2000 is much higher than in 1970 (up 214 percent), that represents annual increase at a rate of only 3.9 percent--which is hardly sufficient to match growth in membership plus inflation. In other words, per member real monetary resources given for Christian work (inflation-adjusted buying power) have not expanded.

Summary evaluations of progress in the various types of Christian ministries are not readily available. As noted earlier, recent emphasis on holistic ministry has led to many new or enlarged endeavors in education, health care, agriculture, literacy, job training, and especially relief and disaster response. Most of these ministries are carried on quietly, with little public notice, but occasionally attracting attention (like Mother Teresa's work among the destitute on the streets of Calcutta).

Creative Approaches

Signs of vitality in the Christian movement do not have to produce formal organizations or large programs. Many are simply local initiatives adapting to changed circumstances. Often a vision comes to one person, who then enlists others to join in a proposed new approach. What begins in a small way may then be copied widely--but still usually without any general organized plan to promote it.

Examples can be cited from many parts of the world. Coffee houses or similar informal meeting places have reached out to alienated youth in cities of the West. In eastern Europe under communism, with church youth activities forbidden, Christians used birthday celebrations as occasions for fellowship and for witness. In India, a group of believers mailed Scripture portions to every home listed in the telephone directories. In tribal areas among illiterates, gospel recordings have been distributed along with small hand-operated players. English classes have been a popular means of contact with persons in many lands. Reading rooms and recreation programs are commonplace.

The "creative access" concept (as noted earlier) has offered hope for avenues of witness to areas closed to traditional missions.

One very promising new method has used chronological Bible "storying" to gain a hearing and to communicate the gospel in pre-literate societies, where stories have a prominent role in both tradition and culture.

Some portions of Christianity do rely heavily on established patterns (and there is value, of course, in tradition), but the Christian faith continues to show great vitality by innovative responses to novel challenges.

7

RELATION TO SOCIETY

Among the matters Latourette examined carefully in his evaluation of Christian progress was the impact of the faith on its environment. Actually, of course, influences would run in both directions. Christianity was affected by its surroundings, as it adapted to the cultures into which it moved. And at the same time, Christians changed their societies in many ways, some only superficial, but some fundamental.

This aspect of advance or decline is not easy to appraise. It does not lend itself readily to quantification, and so David Barrett's research findings can deal with it only tangentially, by summing up Christian activities with potential impact on the world. He can cite the rapid increases in Christian literature, broadcasting, and other ministries, but he has noted that most of these take place in regions that are already predominantly Christian (at least nominally). He has concluded that "most Christian activity does not impact the non-Christian world at all."[70]

There is, indeed, much Christian influence in the world. Most of it perhaps occurs apart from intentional Christian efforts to change things, and often without direct contact. As Western concepts and practices in education and health care, for instance, spread in the non-Western world, they have carry with them attitudes based on Christian principles. Other religions in some cases have imitated what they have seen in Christianity. Christian ideals and standards have had wide acceptance. These processes are hidden and gradual, and so it is virtually impossible to judge their extent in a particular time frame, such as 1970-2000.

Many Christian activities described in earlier chapters involved interaction with society, with resulting effects both on the faith itself and on society. At this point it may be helpful to review some areas of direct involvement in what are often called secular affairs (noting especially events of the past thirty years). Such involvement puts Christian faith in situations where influence on its surroundings may be most likely.

Development and Relief

Commitment to holistic ministry, emphasis on the "option for the poor," increasing participation in development schemes, and growing concern for world hunger and for disaster relief have placed Christians in close contact and cooperation with other social welfare workers and agencies. Church enterprises such as Catholic Relief Services and Church World Service are prominent among the NGOs (non-government organizations) recognized by the United Nations and by many national governments for work in development and relief projects.

Such undertakings are numerous and multi-faceted. Desperate poverty prevails in many countries, and Christians offer help of all kinds. Some examples are emergency food, clothing and shelter in disasters; birth control education; inoculations; literacy courses; well-drilling; agricultural aid; prison ministries; job training; handicraft merchandising; and provision of housing (such as the Habitat for Humanity program).[71]

One of the most impressive recent Christian movements emphasizing social ministries is commonly called neo-evangelical. It was an active minority element at the Lausanne conference in 1974 and has produced a number of influential statements and books since that time. The movement has a strong interest in world hunger--for which it promotes awareness, fund raising, and also lobbying to affect government policies. Ron Sider's 1977 book, *What Do You Say to a Hungry World?*[72] was an important catalyst for Christian involvement with the issue.

Psychological factors cause problems for any human aid effort, both for helpers and for those who are being helped. Helpers encounter the dangers of condescension and pride. Those who receive help may already feel shame because of their need. If help seems impersonal, it may further a sense of worthlessness. Long continued aid often creates attitudes of dependency. Christian aid approaches seek to avoid these difficulties and to preserve and enhance human identity, self-worth, and dignity.[73]

Promotion of Social Justice

There is much kinship and overlapping between ministries of social assistance and action for social change. However, as noted already, controversy over the so-called "social gospel" led to polarization of views earlier in the century. More recently, as Roman Catholics and Protestants in "mainline" denominations emphasized liberation and humanization (largely in terms of social goals), evangelicals became quite distrustful of any attempt to "change the structures of society."

Neo-evangelicals have influenced the views of other

evangelicals, and so there is today less hesitation about political action by Christians in pursuit of more just social systems. All along, Christians of all varieties have supported aid for those in need. More and more have become convinced that it is better, if possible, to prevent or avoid human suffering than simply to minister to those who suffer.[74]

Liberation theology has been geared toward social action for structural change. And political activism has sometimes contributed to major reforms (as in the ending of *apartheid* in South Africa). Conferences on social justice themes and formal position statements have played an important part in Christian promotion of social action.[75] In some cases, Christian groups have associated themselves with representatives of other religions, since they can agree on many ethical values and goals.

A recent example of Christian joint action for social change was the Jubilee 2000 campaign to encourage creditor nations and international lending agencies to reduce or forgive the debts of poverty-stricken Third World nations. Some countries were very unlikely to be able to pay their debts, and even the interest payments were further depleting resources needed for their people's welfare. Though the campaign fell far short of persuading all creditors to forgive the debts, it did have partial success--enough to show the power of concerted Christian action.

Involvement with Religions and Cultures

In the Helsinki Declaration (1975), the international community went on record in support of freedom of religion. In most of the world, that ideal is still far from realization. Actual situations vary greatly. Some countries guarantee full freedom (subject only to balancing the interests of different religious groups, and fitting this freedom in with other legitimate public concerns). Some lands give full liberty to a favored religion, and limit in varying degrees the rights and privileges of others. Other nations have forbidden all religious activities (as in China during the Cultural Revolution, formerly in Albania, and in North Korea under strict communist rule).

Christians interact with society in all these differing settings. At times they suffer persecution. And at times, Christian bodies that represent majority populations, or are favored by government, join in discriminating against or persecuting religious minorities. In the main, the world Christian movement in recent years has fought for increased religious liberty--not only for itself, but for all faiths. That struggle gradually makes progress, though with setbacks from time to time and place to place. Through their share in that effort, Christians are having a positive impact on today's world.

In the process, Christian individuals and organizations develop relationships with government representatives, with prominent citizens in all walks of life, and with leaders of other religions. As in most social interaction, there is influence in both directions. These personal contacts become another avenue for Christian influence in society.

Interfaith dialogue has given further opportunity for Christians to relate in a positive way with non-Christian societies. Though only a small number of Christians and leaders of other faiths participate, such dialogue does help to create an atmosphere of openness, which can lead to easing of inter-religious hostility.

The relation of the Christian faith to culture is quite complex and has been the subject of much study and discussion. Richard Niebuhr's 1951 book, *Christ and Culture*, became a classic.[76] More recently, promotion of contextualization has focused attention on culture. The ancient concept of "Christendom" included an assumption that its cultures were "Christian"--though that was never fully true. To what extent can Christianity be blamed for tragic actions of nominally Christian peoples (warring "tribes" in Rwanda, for example, or in Northern Ireland)? At least it seems appropriate to say that the influence of the faith on those cultures has not been sufficient to prevent the tragedies.

Controversy over the effects of Christian mission on what have been called "primitive" cultures is one expression of the broader question. Secular anthropologists have sometimes accused Christian missions of "cultural imperialism" that endangers such cultures. Don Richardson addressed their criticism in an article, "Do Missionaries Destroy Cultures?"[77] He conceded examples in earlier centuries, but insisted that missionaries are more sensitive today, and actually often form a buffer between such cultures and the political and commercial forces that threaten them.

Lamin Sanneh, an African now on the Yale faculty, has shown the positive cultural results of the spread of Christianity in his perceptive book, *Translating the Message.*[78] He emphasizes the incarnational nature of the Christian faith, which seeks to translate its Scriptures into every language and incorporate its life in every culture. Thus the Christian faith serves as a preserver and strengthener of cultures, not a destroyer. That process has continued in recent decades as the Bible has been translated into more and more languages, and as Christians have emphasized contextualization while seeking to reach every people group.

Regional Evaluation

Any attempt to judge the extent to which Christianity influences its cultural environment (or is influenced by it) is subject to the peril of subjectivism. An estimate by a reasonably informed observer presumably will be at least an educated guess, with the hope that it can be more--but still will be only an individual impression, with which other interpreters may disagree.. Though the hazard is real, the attempt is necessary for our purposes. It must reflect what has been described earlier about the context of the past thirty years, along with the Christian activities and elements of progress already surveyed.

The context has been difficult for religion of any kind--with its new postmodern paradigm, with continuing secularism, with political disturbances and economic change. These have been most evident in the Western world, and many indicators suggest that the influence of Christianity in the West has been declining. Some observers have viewed this as a "post-Christian" era for Europe--which may assess too highly the degree to which Europe was really Christian in earlier generations.

It does seem evident that current European culture is based less on Christian ideals and standards than in the past. Though life in Europe fell far short of being fully Christian, at least lip service was given to the Christian and biblical pattern. Current fading of Europe's traditional allegiance has gone hand in hand with the numerical "defections" from Christian faith cited by Barrett.

As the impact of Christianity on Europe has declined, is the church there influenced more by society than in the past? It is hard to confirm any change. Most of the adaptation of Christian faith to the European setting took place many centuries ago. Today it sometimes seems that the Christian faith lives in its own "ghetto," with minimal influence in either direction.

It has become almost a truism to expect Christianity in North America to follow Europe's example, with a delay of perhaps thirty to fifty years. Though many signs point in that direction, the comparisons are not exact. Church life in America shows considerably more vitality than in the state churches of Europe. But it still is apparently true that the American culture in general is less molded by biblical and Christian norms than in the past. Arts and entertainment, popularized by communications media, have provided norms for a secular society.

Today's culture seems to be effecting more change in the life of American churches than of European. This perhaps simply reflects patterns in America that have never been as firmly traditional as those in Europe's churches.

In Latin America, modernism has eroded the power of the Roman Catholic Church, leading toward a more secular orientation of society. At the same time, evangelicals have multiplied, with an effect on some elements of society, though perhaps not any great influence on the ideals and standards of the culture as a whole. Stan Guthrie, in *Missions in the Third Millennium*, addresses the limited social impact of flourishing evangelical movements in traditional mission fields, describing them as sometimes "a mile wide" but "no more than an inch deep." He diagnoses the problem as superficiality caused by lack of proper discipleship.[79]

The traditional Christian orientation of Latin American culture is retained to a greater degree than in North America, and much more so than in Europe. But political and economic models seem now to be producing more change than religious models.

As to the effects of Latin American society on the church, there seems to be no evident and consistent picture. Social factors (greater freedom, for example) do apparently make it easier today for evangelicals to thrive, and probably at the same time reduce the flow of Catholics into religious vocations. Some changes apparent in Latin America's Catholicism probably flow from Vatican II and not from the cultural environment.

Rapid expansion of Christian faith in Africa has made Christians a majority of the population in many countries. That provides the potential for major influence on society. Other factors in the situation, however, seem to have limited that influence--to the extent that Christianization up to now often appears superficial. More time may be needed before the church in Africa can move beyond a period of being influenced by the culture and enter a period of transforming the culture.

In Asia, as in Africa, Christian faith has been growing rapidly. But the situation overall is quite different. Christians are a majority of the population in only a few places. Venerable cultures with strong religious traditions still determine the ideals and standards of major nations. The possibility that small Christian minorities might change Asia's culture in significant ways is usually quite limited. Some indirect influence, linked with modernization, is observable, but the process is only gradual.

Asia's Christianity definitely has been affected by Asian culture--as the output from Asia's theologians shows clearly. This is part of normal contextualization--unless it goes out of bounds and becomes syncretism. Actually this interaction of Christian faith with the ancient cultures of Asia can help stimulate the church worldwide to rethink the faith for our age, and thus result in great strengthening for the new millennium.

On the whole, what is happening? Is Christianity having a greater impact throughout the world than earlier in the 20th century? Is the faith being changed more by society? It is difficult to conclude that Christian values are now molding the world's thought and practices in any major way. On the contrary, there seems to be some slippage. And the faith itself seems rather to be affected by society, instead of remaking it.

8

ISSUES AND EMPHASES

In addition to those theological and missiological concerns examined already, the Christian faith in recent decades has focused attention on a number of other pressing matters. Some center more in the life of the church itself. Others pertain more to the problems of society. Many of the issues and emphases are inter-connected, and have implications also for theology and for missiology. Several of these special concerns have presented themselves primarily as issues sparking division or controversy in the churches. Others are less controversial, more likely to be identified as prominent Christian themes today.

Issues for the Church

Especially for the Western church, both Catholic and Protestant, the roles and status of women have been a prominent issue. This question to some extent involves and reflects the ongoing interaction of Christian faith with modern life. Generally, in the West, the culture has been moving toward broader opportunities for women. At the same time, churches have been reviewing traditional practices and taking a new look at their biblical and/or doctrinal basis. A 1987 article on "10 Major Trends Facing the Church" cited a shift from male leadership to male/female partnership.[80]

This issue has at times sparked sharp controversy. Should women be ordained as priests in Catholicism or as pastors for Protestants? Some churches and denominations have moved in that direction. Persons conscientiously opposed to the changes have occasionally withdrawn and formed separate denominations. Most situations have not reached that extreme--but the problems are still unresolved and continue to stir discussion and friction. The opposing views both claim to be grounded in biblical principles and/or historic doctrinal positions.

Other current issues, though not as prevalent, center in the family and human sexuality. Especially critical is the church's response to homosexuality. However, there are other questions arising from changing family mores in Western culture--divorce and its effects on families, premarital and extramarital sex (including cohabiting without marriage), abortion, pornography, abuse of children--and, for Roman Catholics, contraception and clerical celibacy. On some of these questions there may be fairly general Christian agreement as to basic principles, but differences as to how best to cope with the problems involved.

Conflicting views of "evangelism" in contrast with "proselytism" have been a further area of discussion and occasional dissension in the relationships of churches. Though this issue is by no means new, it became especially pertinent in the 1990s, following the new freedom in eastern Europe and the former Soviet Union, as Protestant and evangelical mission agencies moved into areas with strong Orthodox traditions.

A further issue in the life of the churches has been an ongoing debate on appropriate relations between church and state.

Christians themselves hold to no consistent position on the question. Some believe in complete separation of church and state. Others support various kinds of cooperation between the two. And many favor an established state church. Since government policies also differ so widely, this issue will no doubt continue to challenge the church on into the next century.

Emphases in the Life of the Church

Worship lies at the very heart of the church's life. And the past thirty years have witnessed much innovation in the worship of Western churches--along with much wider acceptance of varying cultural forms of worship in other parts of the world.

The burgeoning charismatic movement has played a prominent part in changing patterns of worship. But elements of Western culture, such as the music preferences of youth and the influence of television, have had their influence too. Myriads of churches have begun offering less formal services, sometimes described as "seeker-sensitive," intended to appeal to young outsiders.

A more recent and less prominent trend has renewed interest in liturgical worship, most notably in a revival of Celtic forms.

Outside the Western world, and in tune with modern emphasis on ethnicity, the relatively new field of ethnomusicology has gained wide recognition and support. During the long history of the modern mission movement, Western music was translated into local languages, but retaining its musical forms. It tended to become the accepted musical style of Christians--though often entirely foreign to their own culture. Now Christians in many lands are developing contextualized musical styles.

Prayer has been receiving unusual attention and emphasis. Some new Christian organizations have prayer as their exclusive purpose, and many existing agencies have added a prayer office or a prayer leader to their staffs. Numerous speakers and writers have focused on prayer as "spiritual warfare." A further aspect of the prayer emphasis is the novel concept of "prayer-walking"--which involves usually a small group of Christians walking around in a community and praying along the way for persons and situations encountered. It intends to be unobtrusive, while sensitizing Christians to the needs of the community, and making their prayers more specific and graphic.

Prayer has been prominent in the mission efforts aimed at unreached peoples, and especially in the plans of the AD 2000 Movement. Ralph Winter already in the 1970s was promoting an "Adopt-a-People" concept, with prayer for the people group as a central element. By 1995, the AD 2000 Movement sponsored a month of concerted prayer by "Great Commission Christian groups" for the peoples of the "10/40 Window," with 100 cities of that region identified as "gateway cities" for which to pray during the month.

A prominent denominational leader a few years ago, calling himself "only a layman," promoted the idea of "abolishing the laity." He was emphasizing the point, increasingly accepted among evangelicals, that the traditional clergy/laity division has little clear basis in Scripture. More broadly in the church, the place of lay persons is being given new significance. The 1987 article cited earlier, on "10 Major Trends Facing the Church," included a trend from clergy/laity to a "community of ministers."[81] This current trend seems likely to continue and to add new vitality to the Christian movement.

In Western and especially in North American Christianity, churches recently have tended to adopt secular models for their organization and activities. Corporate structures, with planning systems based often on "management by objectives," have become a common pattern for churches and for para-church agencies. This tendency as evidenced in mission agencies has been described as "managerial missiology."[82]

In today's world, communication is an especially common and prominent concern--and certainly no less so in the church. Skills in public relations are highly valued. All the modern technologies for communication are utilized. Promotion of church programs and projects uses the many formulas seen in commercial advertising. This Western trend toward corporate methods has influenced Westernized segments of non-Western Christianity, but is rejected on cultural grounds (and perhaps spiritual also) by much of the non-Western church.

Concerns for Society

Several current Christian emphases go beyond the inner life of the church, to deal with important questions and problems of modern society. Christians, of course, are not alone in seeking solutions to critical world problems, but find themselves involved with many other forces (governmental, religious, and secular). Christian attention to these matters in most cases predated 1970, but the severity of the situations and/or the intensity of Christian interest has grown remarkably in recent decades.

Ecology has become an especially urgent theme, bringing new

appreciation for biblical teaching about God's creation and human stewardship. The church has responded to warnings from science about threats to the environment, and has sought to sensitize the consciences of its own members, and to raise its voice in support of action to help preserve our world. Dangers cited include depletion of natural resources; deforestation, erosion, and desertification; endangering of animal and plant species; and pollution of soil, water , and air (with possible harm to the ozone shield, a "greenhouse effect," and global warming). An increasing chorus of Christian speakers and writers has addressed these challenges.[83]

Human welfare and especially public health needs have received growing Christian attention (in accord with the holistic emphasis in theology and missiology described earlier). Such concerns are presented vividly in *Target Earth* (published in 1989), with tables and diagrams on childhood deaths; comparative mortality rates and life expectancy; poverty, with shortages of food, shelter, and energy; and some major hazards for human life and well-being.[84]

Since 1981, Acquired Immunodeficiency Syndrome (AIDS) has become a tragic and rapidly spreading plague worldwide, but with special severity in Africa. Christian response at first was equivocal, with some wishing to avoid the issue, and some passing judgment on the victims. Most Christians have become sympathetic and many are ministering to persons infected with HIV (the virus identified as the cause of AIDS). This scourge poses a grave challenge to the Christian movement in Africa.

A problem centered mainly in the West is that of substance abuse. The church is heavily engaged in ministries seeking to confront the drug culture that ravages inner cities and spreads its poison in youth sub-cultures--and seeking also to rescue its casualties. Such efforts are not new, but great creativity goes into devising Christian programs to overcome this and other cultural enemies of abundant human life (enemies such as pornography, gambling, alcoholism, and escalating violence).

Long before 1970, Christians were in the forefront of workers for world peace. The peace movement as an organized force may be less evident than it was earlier, now that the Cold War has ended, but Christians are a vital part of peace efforts in many scattered conflict areas. Increasingly Christian statesmen seek to be peace-makers in situations of hostility (an example is the mediation roles of former United States president Jimmy Carter).

The continuing struggle for human rights has been another arena of Christian action. The ways in which Christians can engage in such efforts are conditioned, in different parts of the world, by their varying circumstances. Though Christians have tended to major on religious liberty, they have contended also in many cases for fundamental human freedoms as a matter of principle. Some segments of Christianity at times have begrudged to others the liberty they desired for themselves--but the main trend in recent Christian thought, speech, writing, and activity supports the concept of full freedom for all persons everywhere.

Racism continues to disturb and challenge today's world, with distressing outbreaks of genocidal strife in the past three decades. In several places, population groups claiming Christian faith have taken part in the violence against other groups. In many places, Christians are the targets of discrimination or violence. On the total world scene, Christian leaders have condemned racism and are working toward its elimination.

In this increasingly urban world, Christian ministries addressed to cities and their people have multiplied, involving numerous conferences and strategic studies of all aspects of urban life, and scores of new books. This obviously has been another important emphasis in current Christianity--and not limited to the Western world, as megacities have mushroomed in all parts of the world. International Urban Associates is an organization formed to help Christians worldwide in their planning for urban ministries.

Many segments of world Christianity, for a variety of reasons (both doctrinal and circumstantial), involve themselves only minimally with the broader communities in which they live. But the trend continues toward greater involvement, through the emphases just reviewed and through others more limited or local.

CONCLUSION: ANALYSIS AND OUTLOOK

We have been surveying the condition of the world Christian movement between 1970 and 2000. These have been dramatic and momentous years both for humanity and for the church, with many startling changes. We return now to questions raised at the start: In these thirty years, has Christianity been advancing or declining? Can the period still be considered an extension of "advance through storm" (as Latourette labeled the years from 1914 to 1944)? If so, that seems a good description for the entire 20th century.

In analyzing what the record shows, we would not want to deceive ourselves by viewing it "through rose-colored glasses," overlooking or downplaying Christian faults and failings. The church as an empirical actuality is deeply flawed, subject to all the hazards of individual human fallibility and sinfulness and to the temptations typical of institutions. In the events of church history we can see always the hand of God, but we see also a large measure of merely human attitudes and actions--and at times clearly demonic elements. Christians in the period we have examined were not exempt from these realities.

Historical analysis is inevitably subjective. Any author will be limited in knowledge and in sources of information, will approach the subject from some distinctive personal background and perspective, and certainly will be capable of lapses in judgment. This author can present only his own best evaluation of what has taken place, basing it on the information available to him, as set forth in the preceding chapters. Another analyst, of course, with additional sources or a differing perspective, might come to other conclusions.

Review of Latourette's Criteria

In his seven-volume master work, *A History of the Expansion of Christianity*,[85] and in his other books reflecting the same research, Kenneth Scott Latourette described alternating periods of advance and retreat by the Christian faith. His analysis made use of four main criteria--numerical growth or decline, geographical spread or retreat, evidences of vitality or of dormancy, and extent of influence on society. These same criteria can serve for an evaluation of Christianity from 1970 to 2000.

The number of Christians (by David Barrett's broad definition) obviously has grown dramatically--increasing 61.7 percent in thirty years. However, as noted earlier, that growth has not quite kept pace with an expanding world population. As a percentage of humanity, the Christian faith represented only 33 percent in 2000 by contrast with 33.5 percent in 1970.

Primary reasons for the declining ratio seem to be the relatively lower birth rates in traditionally Christian nations, and defections from Christianity in the highly secularized West. Rapid numerical gains in Africa and Asia have not been sufficient to offset the slower growth in other regions.

It remains true that the losses have occurred mainly among those often called nominal Christians or cultural Christians, while the gains have come largely in more vigorous segments of the faith. Evangelicals, charismatics, and those Barrett labels "Great Commission Christians" have grown at rates exceeding that of world population.

Geographical spread of Christianity has continued and in some respects accelerated. With a shift in "center of gravity" of the faith from its traditional heartland in Europe and North America to the non-Western world, Christianity has become more aptly a world religion. Though some observers have suggested that the missionary era has ended, the number of workers and the range of mission efforts has expanded, with a large non-Western contingent added to the mix. And recent emphasis on outreach to neglected people groups has helped fill in some gaps in the map showing the locations of Christians.

Despite the expansion of the past thirty years, there are still vast areas and population groups where Christians are few--represented largely by the so-called "10-40 Window." But the overall picture has been one of steady geographical advance.

Chapter 6 has reviewed the widespread and multi-faceted expressions of vitality of the Christian faith in recent years. There are still some segments of the faith that seem bound by tradition, hampered by harsh environments, or weak and torpid. But such situations are outside the mainstream. Judging by the vitality criterion, the faith as a whole has certainly been moving ahead.

Chapter 7 reviewed the influence of Christianity on society, and also the extent to which the Christian faith was itself influenced by its cultural settings. As noted there, such effects are difficult to evaluate. Between 1970 and 2000, on the whole and relative to preceding decades, Christian influence seemed diminished. Secular worldviews and values increasingly dominated regions whose historic cultures had been most distinctively Christian. In Africa and Asia, where the Christian faith was spreading and growing most rapidly, and was demonstrating unusual vigor, it was often a minority without enough power to effect major change in the culture of the majority.

To sum up: The Christian faith was spreading, not retreating. Though the number of its nominal adherents was not keeping pace with world population, its central core of committed believers was growing much more rapidly. Vitality demonstrated by the faith was impressive. Only its influence on society fell short of that in earlier generations. In all, the period 1970-2000 must be judged as a time of further advance for Christianity on the world scene.

Continuing Advance Through Storm?

It is interesting to speculate how Latourette might interpret the 20th century if he were completing his study now, rather than in 1944. Would he treat the years from 1914 to the end of the century as a unit, still called "Advance Through Storm"? The periods into which Latourette divided the history of Christian expansion were usually much longer than the merely 30 years included in his final volume. I believe he would have seen the years from 1914 to 2000 as one period. Would it have had still the same title?

Ralph Winter's survey covering 1945-1969 (entitled *The Twenty-Five Unbelievable Years*[86]) reports considerable "storm." In a chapter on "The Retreat of the West," he examines the ending of Western colonialism and the struggles of new nations. Those years were also the height of the Cold

War, with hot wars in Korea and in Vietnam. Major turbulence enveloped China, with transition to a communist regime, and with the excesses of the Cultural Revolution.

The final three decades of the century have seemed less stormy. China moved beyond its period of great repression. The Soviet Union disbanded, and its "colonies" gained their freedom. The Cold War came to an end. Local conflicts, however, continued to threaten world peace--with the Middle East the most troubled region, and with Arab-Israeli tensions apparently intractable.

Though political and military troubles diminished, the Christian faith had to contend with new challenges--rapid social and cultural change, burgeoning populations and thronging cities, and economic globalization. The scourge of AIDS spread itself around the globe. A postmodern paradigm threatened to reduce all religious faiths to mere personal notions. And a revived and aggressive Islam began promoting itself as a potential world faith. Perhaps Latourette would see reason enough to consider the entire 20th century a time of continuing storm for Christians.

Winter's book proclaimed 1945-1969 as years of "unbelievable" advance for Christianity. The period 1970-2000 was summarized above as one of continuing (though perhaps less spectacular) progress. Thus it can be appropriate to designate the entire century as one of advance through storm.

The End of the Millennium

The year 2000 completed the second millennium of Christian history. Though the calendar has no ultimate significance, its changes do become landmarks in human experience. Thus it is appropriate to examine the position of the Christian faith after two thousand years.

The thirty years of mixed gains and losses just reviewed bring Christianity to a situation of new strengths and of new trials.

The church has acquired a fresh vision of world evangelization, reflected in the Global Evangelization Movement described earlier, and in the AD 2000 organization that embodied the vision. Its objectives entailed increased awareness of "unreached peoples" and a commitment to communicate the gospel to every such group. These and other new strategic emphases enable the church to respond more fully to the needs of the world.

The events leading up to the close of the 20th century brought great new opportunities for Christian evangelism and ministry. The decline of communism in the Soviet Union and its client states opened many avenues of outreach. New freedom for Christian missions extended to such widely scattered lands as Ethiopia, Angola, and Mozambique in Africa; Albania in Europe; and Nepal, Cambodia, and Mongolia in Asia.

Many areas and many peoples formerly resistant to the Christian message have begun to show new responsiveness. That is true of many tribes being addressed through the emphasis on people groups. On a vastly larger scale, it has been true in China, where tens of millions had come to faith in Christ by the century's close.

New resources have become available to help spread the Christian faith. These include the marvels of technology for gathering and analyzing information, for communication, and for transportation. The Bible is being translated into ever more and more languages, with 80 percent of the world's people by AD 2000 having the Scriptures available in a language they understand. David Barrett in his *World Christian Encyclopedia* cites impressive increases in Christian literature and broadcasts. The *Jesus* film produced by Campus Crusades has become available in more than 500 languages. The most promising new resources for Christian advance are the hundreds of mission agencies and the many thousands of new missionaries originating from the Third World.

In telling the story of Christianity toward the close of the millennium, we have described prominent persons and decisive movements--but there is another untold and indeed untellable story. Behind the public events and movements, there have been the countless myriads of unknown and unheralded believers whose lives of faith have made the entire story possible. Those are the ultimate resource for the Christian movement.

Over against these strengths of the Christian movement, the turn-of-century context includes major difficulties. In a 1996 book, Samuel Huntington suggested that "the post-Cold War world is being divided along religious and cultural fault lines."[87] This evident reality is breeding restrictive governments, aggressive religions and cultures, and increasingly prevalent secularism. Despite changes which seem to make the Christian task simpler, the confrontation of Christian faith with obstacles in today's world may be even more intense than it was in 1970.

Prospect for the New Millennium

It has been suggested that Christians need now to think of AD 2000 not as a target, but as "a new launch point."[88]

Investment advisers are required to state that past performance is no guarantee of future results. That is true in all of life, not merely in financial matters. We would like to know the future of the Christian movement, and projecting trends from the past is always tempting. But trends do not automatically continue.

We can report with some confidence the advance of the Christian faith in the 20th century, including its final decades (tempered, of course, by an awareness of some failings). But we cannot presume what the events of the future will be, whether favorable or threatening to the Christian movement--or just how Christians will respond to those conditions. We still "walk by faith, not by sight" (2 Cor. 5:7).

Several things, however, can be said with assurance about the new millennium. Most important is the sure word about God and His purpose: "The earth will be filled with the knowledge of the glory of the Lord, as the waters cover the sea" (Hab. 2:114). While God allows the world to stand, He intends to challenge His people toward the evangelizing of the entire human race, and to guide, empower, and bless in that process. The history of the expansion of Christianity is a continuing story!

Two further words: We must expect the unexpected. No one could have predicted the astounding changes that took place in the past thirty years, and we cannot imagine what changes await us now. Furthermore, by the power of God's Holy Spirit, the Christian faith has the vitality to respond to whatever the future brings. We can call the 20th century to give its testimony to that vitality. And we can rely on the promise of Jesus to His church, as it carries out its task of "discipling all the nations," that He will be with it " to the very end of the age" (Matt. 28:20).

Notes

[1]. Kenneth Scott Latourette, *A history of the Expansion of Christianity, Vol. 1-7* (New York: Harper and Brothers, 1937-1945).

[2]. Ralph D. Winter, *The Twenty-Five Unbelievable Years, 1945-1969* (Pasadena, CA: William Carey Library, 1970).

[3]. *Op.cit.,* title of Chapter 1.

[4]. Larry D. Pate describes the problem in *From Every People* (Monrovia, CA: MARC, 1989), pp. 12-14.

[5]. David B. Barrett *et al.*, ed., *World Christian Encyclopedia*, Second Edition, (London: Oxford University Press, 2001), Global Table 1-1, vol. 1, p. 4.

[6]. Paul Ehrlich, *The Population Bomb* (New York: Ballantine, 1968).

[7]. David B. Barrett, *World-Class Cities and World Evangelization* (Birmingham, AL: New Hope, 1986), p. 16.

[8]. For an extended description of this process, see Winston Crawley, *Global Mission* (Nashville: Broadman Press, 1985), pp. 54-56.

[9]. For a brief overview, see Crawley, *op.cit.*, pp. 56-57.

[10]. Barrett, *World Christian Encyclopedia, ibid.*

[11]. The conference was sponsored by the Commission on World Mission and Evangelism of the World Council of Churches, with the theme "Salvation Today." Evangelicals criticized interpreting salvation as "humanization."

[12]. For an interpretation, see Crawley, *op.cit.*, 254-257.

[13]. Alvin Toffler, *Future Shock* (New York: Random House, 1970).

[14]. Alvin Toffler, *The Third Wave* (New York: William Morrow, 1980).

[15]. John Naisbitt, *Megatrends* (New York: Warner, 1982).

[16]. *Change: Threat or Opportunity*, 5 volumes (New York: United Nations Publications, 1992).

[17]. Paul R. and Anne H. Ehrlich, *The Population Explosion* (New York: Simon & Schuster, 1990).

[18]. *World-Class Cities, loc.cit.*

[19]. *Op.cit.*, pp. 48-49 and 10.

[20]. Many details in this section and those that follow rely on J. M. Roberts, *Twentieth Century: The History of the World, 1901-2000* (New York: Viking, 1999) and on Michael Howard and Wm. Roger Louis, eds., *The Oxford History of the Twentieth Century* (New York: Oxford University Press, 1998).

[21]. Produced by the Population Crisis Committee, 1120 19th Street N.W., Washington, D.C. 20036.

[22]. Second Edition (2000), vol. 1, p. 6.

[23]. (Pasadena, CA: Global Mapping International, 1989), pp. 30-55.

[24]. Ingomar Hauchler and Paul M. Kennedy, eds., *Global Trends: The World Almanac of Development and Peace* (New York: Continuum, 1994), p. 329.

[25]. *World Christian Encyclopedia*, Second Edition, vol. 1, p. 28.

[26]. *Op.cit.,* vol. 1, p. 3. World data that follow are from page 10, and country data from sections for specific countries.

[27]. *International Bulletin of Missionary Research,* Jan. 1985, p. 30.

[28]. *Op.cit.,* Jan. 1987, p.24.

[29]. *World Christian Encyclopedia, Second Edition,* Volume 1, p. 11.

[30]. See Stan Guthrie, *Missions in the Third Millennium* (Waynesboro, GA: Paternoster Press, 2000), pp. 181-183.

[31]. Walbert Buhlmann, *The Church of the Future* (Maryknoll, NY: Orbis Books, 1986), pp. 4-5 (published originally in German in 1981) .

[32]. Gerald H. Anderson and Thomas F. Stransky, eds., *Mission Trends No. 3: Third World Theologies* (New York: Paulist Press, 1976), p. 1.

[33]. C. Peter Wagner, *Stop the World I Want to Get On,* excerpted by Marlin L. Nelson, ed., *Readings in Third World Missions* (Pasadena, CA: William Carey Library, 1976), p. 58.

[34]. Nelson, *op.cit.*, pp. 102-103.

[35]. Lawrence E. Keyes, *The Last Age of Missions: A Study of Third World Missionary Societies* (Pasadena, CA: William Carey Library, 1983).

[36]. Larry D. Pate, *From Every People* (Monrovia, CA: MARC, 1989).

[37]. David J. Bosch, *Transforming Mission* (Maryknoll, NY: Orbis Books, 1991), pp. 262-274 (quotations from p. 262).

[38]. *Op.cit.*, pp. 349-362.

[39]. Donald McGavran, ed., *The Conciliar-Evangelical Debate: The Crucial Documents, 1964-1976* (Pasadena, CA: William Carey Library, 1977).

[40]. See, for example, Waldron Scott, *Bring Forth Justice: A contemporary Perspective on Mission* (Grand Rapids, MI: Eerdmans, 1980).

[41]. Bosch, *op.cit.*, p. 462.

[42]. Quoted by Arthur F. Glasser in *Contemporary Theologies of Mission* (Grand Rapids, MI: Baker Book House, 1983), p. 175.

[43]. In an essay on "Changes in Roman Catholic Attitudes toward Proselytism and Mission," in James A Scherer and Stephen B. Bevans, *New Directions in Mission and Evangelization 2* , (Maryknoll, NY: Orbis Books, 1994), pp. 113-125.

[44]. Bosch, *op.cit.*, p. 474.

[45]. Bosch, *op.cit.*, treats the entire question at length in a section on "Witness to People of Other Living Faiths" (pp. 474-489).

[46]. George Brunk, III, in his essay on "The Exclusiveness of Jesus Christ," in *New Directions in Mission and Evangelization 2*.

[47]. Bosch, *op.cit.*, p.384.

[48]. See the "Antecedents" section (pp. 150-154) of a chapter on liberation theology by Arthur F. Glasser in *Contemporary Theologies of Mission.*

[49]. Bosch, *op.cit.*, "From Development to Liberation" (pp.432-435), in his lengthy section on "Mission as Liberation" (pp. 432-447).

[50]. Glasser, *op.cit.*, p. 164.

[51]. *Op.cit.*, pp. 498-499.

[52]. Hal Lindsey, *The Late Great Planet Earth* (Grand Rapids: Zondervan, 1970).

[53]. Johannes Verkuyl, *Contemporary Missiology* (Grand Rapids: Eerdmans, 1978), pp. 197-198; Orlando E. Costas, *Christ Outside the Gate: Mission Beyond Christendom* (Maryknoll, NY: Orbis Books, 1982), pp. 91ff.; Glasser, *op.cit.*, pp. 30-46. For further examples, see Winston Crawley, *op.cit.*, pp. 80-83,

[54]. The process is traced by Johannes Verkuyl, *op.cit.*, pp. 1-17; and by David Bosch, *op.cit.*, pp. 489-498. They describe also the content and roles of missiology and its relation to other disciplines.

[55]. Edward R. Dayton and David A. Fraser, *Planning Strategies for World Evangelization* (Grand Rapids: Eerdmans, 1980).

[56]. Donald Anderson McGavran, *The Bridges of God* (London: World Dominion Press, 1955).

[57]. *How Churches Grow* (London: World Dominion Press, 1959); and *Understanding Church Growth* (Grand Rapids: Eerdmans, 1970).

[58]. See the conference report: Allan Starling, ed., *Seeds of Promise* (Pasadena, CA: William Carey Library, 1981).

[59]. See Jay and Olgy Gary, eds., *The Countdown Has begun* (Rockville, VA: AD 2000 Global Service Office, 1989).

[60]. See the May-June 1995 issue of *Mission Frontiers*.

[61]. Ramifications of contextualization are examined in Bosch, *op.cit.*, pp.420-432; Crawley, *op.cit.*, pp. 202-205; and Wilbert R. Shenk, *Changing Frontiers of Mission* (Maryknoll, NY: Orbis Books, 1999), pp. 56-58. Bosch makes a somewhat obscure distinction between contextualization and inculturation.

[62]. *The Willowbank Report* (Wheaton, IL: Lausanne Committee for World Evangelization, 1978).

[63]. For reports from the conference, see Virgil Gerber, ed., *Missions in Creative Tension* (Pasadena, CA: William Carey Library, 1971) and

C. Peter Wagner, ed., *Church/Mission Tensions Today* (Chicago: Moody Press, 1972). A more recent book on the same subject is W. Harold Fuller, *Mission--Church Dynamics* (Pasadena, CA: William Carey Library, 1980).

64. For an overview, see the July-August 1994 issue of *Mission Frontiers*.

65. C. Peter Wagner, *Look Out! The Pentecostals Are Coming* (Carol Stream, IL: Creation House, 1973).

66. *World Christian Encyclopedia*, Second Edition, Vol. 1, p. 19.

67. *Op.cit.*, p.4.

68. *International Bulletin of Missionary Research*, January, 2000, p. 24.

69. Comparisons that follow reflect data in the *World Christian Encyclopedia*, Second Edition, Volume 1, Table 5-1, but more easily available from the *International Bulletin of Missionary Research*, January, 2001, p. 25.

70. In a report on "measuring the Christian impact," related to his annual statistical update in the *International Bulletin of Missionary Research,* January, 1997, p. 24.

71. For brief summary treatments, see "State of World Need" in Ralph D. Winter and Steven C. Hawthorne, eds., *Perspectives on the World Christian Movement*, Third Edition (Pasadena, CA: William Carey Library, 1999), pp. 569-574; and Gordon Aeschliman, *Global-Trends* (Downers Grove, IL: InterVarsity Press, 1990), pp. 35-42.

72. Revised and updated as *Rich Christians in an Age of Hunger* (Dallas: Word, 1997).

73. See a chapter on the work of Vinay Samuel along that line, in Vinay Samuel and Chris Sugden, *A.D. 2000 and Beyond: A Mission Agenda* (Oxford: Regnum Books, 1991), pp. 56-81.

74. See the chapter on "Mission as Action for God's Justice," by Lesslie Newbigin, in *The Open Secret* (Grand Rapids: Eerdmans, 1978), pp. 102-134.

75. For examples of such statements, see the Oxford Declaration on Christian Faith and Economics, in Aeschliman, *op.cit.*, pp. 117-141; and the report of the Third Latin American Congress on Evangelism, in Scherer and Bevans, *op.cit.*, pp. 191-198.

[76]. H. Richard Niebuhr, *Christ and Culture* (New York: Harper, 1951).

[77]. Included in *Perspectives on the World Christian Movement*, Third Edition, pp. 460-468.

[78]. Lamin O. Sanneh, *Translating the Message* (Maryknoll, NY: Orbis Books, 1989).

[79]. Guthrie, *op.cit.*, p. 147.

[80]. Howard A. Snyder and Daniel B. Runyon , in the *International Bulletin of Missionary Research*, April, 1987.

[81]. *Op.cit.*

[82] Guthrie, *op.cit.*, p. 162.

[83]. See, for example, Frank Caleb Jansen, ed., *Target Earth* (Pasadena, CA: Global Mapping International, 1989), pp. 36-41, 56-63; and Aeschliman, *op.cit.*, chapter 4.

[84]. Jansen, *op.cit.*, under various topics in sections on mankind, the basic human needs, and threats.

[85]. Kenneth Scott Latourette, *A History of the Expansion of Christianity, Vol. 1-7* (New York: Harper and Brothers, 1937-1945).

[86]. Ralph D. Winter, *The Twenty-Five Unbelievable Years, 1945-1969* (Pasadena, CA: William Cary Library, 1970).

[87]. See Guthrie, *op.cit.*, p. 168, citing Huntington's *The Clash of Civilizations and the Remaking of World Order* (New York: Simon and Schuster, 1996).

[88]. *Op.cit.*, p. 192, quoting Jay Gary, director of the Christian Futures Network.